ADRISHYA

Launched in November 2014, **EPIC Television Channel** is India's leading factual entertainment platform. An India-centric content-driven destination, EPIC has redefined the infotainment genre by being the only native Hindi language medium in its league. The channel has been bestowed with several accolades, including the prestigious 12 PromaxBDA Award across various categories as well as the Indian Television Academy Award for the show 'Stories by Rabindranath Tagore'. Famed for its inaugural history and focus on mythology, EPIC has recently elevated its brand proposition and now showcases a wide array of original content across various genres. This critically acclaimed channel has expanded the scope of its offerings by including within its programming repertoire an eclectic mix of non-fiction content that aspires to imbibe the diversity of India.

EPIC has an extensive catalogue of original programming and a reputation for excellence in premium factual content that celebrates, explores, discovers and inspires India through untold stories, facts and possibilities—a channel which tells the story of the people, for the people and by the people of India.

ADRISHYA

True Stories of Indian Spies

Published by
Rupa Publications India Pvt. Ltd 2017
7/16, Ansari Road, Daryaganj
New Delhi 110002

Sales centres:
Allahabad Bengaluru Chennai
Hyderabad Jaipur Kathmandu
Kolkata Mumbai

Copyright © EPIC Television Pvt. Ltd. 2017
All images courtesy © EPIC Television Pvt. Ltd.
Transcreated by Chandni Mathur

The views and opinions expressed in this book are the author's own and the facts are as reported by him which have been verified to the extent possible, and the publishers are not in any way liable for the same.

All rights reserved.

No part of this publication may be reproduced, transmitted, or stored in a retrieval system, in any form or by any means, electronic, mechanical, photocopying, recording or otherwise, without the prior permission of the publisher.

ISBN: 978-81-291-4810-0

First impression 2017

10 9 8 7 6 5 4 3 2 1

Printed and bound in India by Repro Knowledgecast Limited, Thane

This book is sold subject to the condition that it shall not, by way of trade or otherwise, be lent, resold, hired out, or otherwise circulated, without the publisher's prior consent, in any form of binding or cover other than that in which it is published.

Contents

Prologue   *vii*

Kacha   1
The Spy of the Gods

Jeev Siddhi   19
Chanakya's Spy

Chand Bardai   38
The Poet Spy

Bahirji Naik   58
Chhatrapati Shivaji Maharaj's Chief Intelligence Officer

Sharan Kaur   81
The Warrior Spy

Aziz-Un-Nisa   103
The Courtesan Spy

Durga Bhabhi 124
The Revolutionary Spy

Noor Inayat Khan 145
The Unlikely Spy

Saraswati Rajamani 167
Netaji's Spy

Rameshwar N. Kao and K. Shankaran Nair 191
RAW Spies and the 1971 War

Prologue

This book is based on EPIC Television's popular show by the same name—'Adrishya: True Stories of Indian Spies'. It features select stories of the greatest Indian spies from the times of the Mahabharata to RAW spies during the Bangladesh Liberation War in 1971, and many other interesting ones in between.

Adrishya: True Stories of Indian Spies makes you experience life from the point of view of India's greatest spies, living through danger and possible death, fear and anxiety, the triumphs and the captures. It narrates the spies' heroic acts and follows them as they travel through dangerous landscapes, slip into disguises and hoodwink the enemy. We become privy to their thoughts as they inch towards fulfilling their mission.

Featuring stories from different eras, the book

begins with a lesser-known tale from the master of all epics—Mahabharata. Guru Brihaspati's son Kacha, the spy of the gods, was sent by Lord Indra to learn mrit sanjeevani vidya from Guru Shukracharya, a knowledge which would make the gods immortal. While he achieved his mission, it came with a heavy price.

Next is Jeev Siddhi, Chanakya's spy. He assisted his guru Chanakya in saving Chandragupta Maurya's life and expand his kingdom by strategically defeating King Nanda's minister, Rakshasa.

The work of a spy can be varied. They need not always be warriors. Like Chand Bardai—who served under Prithviraj Chauhan, the king of the Hindu Chauhan dynasty that ruled over Ajmer and Delhi—was a court poet, a jester and a master of disguises. Faithful to his master, Bardai was involved in helping Chauhan's beloved Sanyukta escape from Kannauj on the day of her swayamvar. Later, when Prithviraj Chauhan was blinded and imprisoned by Mohammad Ghori of Ghazni, Bardai plotted a way for Chauhan to seek revenge from the cruel Ghori.

Bahirji Naik, Chhatrapati Shivaji's chief intelligence officer, was a master of disguises and one of the early practitioners of a form of guerrilla warfare called Ganimi Kawa or Shiva Sutra.

PROLOGUE

Then there is Sharan Kaur, who was saved by the army of Hari Singh Nalwa, the great commander of the Sikh empire of Maharaja Ranjit Singh. She returned the favour by becoming a warrior spy, helping Nalwa counter the ferocious attacks of the Pathan tribes and their cruel leader Dost Mohammad. Sharan braved to go where no Sikh man would go.

Aziz-Un-Nisa's and Durga Bhabhi's stories are of exemplary courage. Aziz-Un, a courtesan, who had travelled from the cultural city of Lucknow to the gritty reality of Kanpur, just to maintain the independence of her choices, turned against the British and started out as a spy. But after the British killed the man she loved, she didn't hesitate from actively participating in the planning of the uprising of 1857. Durga Bhabhi is another revolutionary Indian woman spy. Married to a freedom fighter at the age of eleven, Durgavati Vohra was actively involved in the planning and execution of several of the Hindustan Socialist Republican Army's (HSRA) activities. She is best known for having travelled undercover with Bhagat Singh when the British police was on the lookout for him in relation to the murder of Saunders.

The story of Noor Inayat Khan is equally interesting. A Sufi poet, a princess by birth and a children's author,

Noor, despite her Sufi background, becomes the sole link between the rebel groups of France and their support system in England during World War II. How she gets into the elite secret services of Women's Auxiliary Air Force (WAAF) accounts for a fascinating story.

Saraswati Rajamani was Netaji Subhash Chandra Bose's spy in the Indian National Army (INA). Saraswati joined the INA at a young age and infiltrated British army ranks to gather intelligence for Netaji which helped him in his active resistance to the British Raj. The story also captures her escape when she was caught by the British forces.

The story of the creation of Bangladesh is incomplete without the mention of two Indian intelligence officers, R.N. Kao and K. Shankar Nair. While Kao planned meticulously from Research and Analysis Wing (RAW) headquarters in New Delhi, K. Shankar Nair was on the field as the freedom struggle in East Pakistan raged. The chapter details their heroic deed in saving countless lives and achieving freedom for India's neighbouring country.

These myriad cases give us a glimpse into the dangerous lives of the unsung heroes of wars while reaffirming the importance of their roles in the safety and security of the nation. These are stories that will inspire and entertain at the same time.

PROLOGUE

The information in these chapters is based on critical inputs provided by scholars and experts for the TV show. In a few chapters, the spies, who are still among us, have shared their experiences too. This book doesn't claim to be a history book but gives us an insight into the lives of spies, told in these very interesting story formats.

1
Kacha

The Spy of the Gods
(Adi Parva, Mahabharata)

Kacha's story is from a time when both gods and demons were mortals, existing as warring tribes. Then one day, the preceptor of the demons (asuras), Shukracharya, was blessed with the knowledge of mrit sanjeevani which he used to bring dead demons back to life. Blessed with immortality, the demons became invincible and the power of gods (devas) came under severe threat. To learn the secret that had been bringing their enemies back to life, Brihaspati, the guru of the devas, sent his son Kacha into the land of the asuras. Unlike any other spy, Kacha walked into enemy territory as himself, risking his life to fulfil his promise made to the devas. However, when Shukracharya's daughter Devyani fell in love with him, Kacha realized that perhaps the only way he could gain the knowledge of immortality would be through his own death.

In Indian mythology, the gods or devas used to live in the Devlok, while the demons or the asuras used to live all over the universe, in all three dimensions, and create a ruckus. They were a mischievous lot. The devas and asuras were completely opposite to each other; the gods were cultured, thoughtful and decent, while the demons were thought to be vandals who would always create havoc and trouble others.

According to the legend of the Saptarishi, there were seven rishis who were the beholder of all knowledge in the universe. Rishi Angiras and Rishi Bhrigu were a part of Saptarishi. Brihaspati was the son of Rishi Angiras and Shukracharya was the son of Rishi Bhrigu. When Shukracharya grew up and the time came for his education, he went to sage Angiras and started his education under him. It was not known whether he did so out of his own choice or on the advice of his father. He used to study at Angiras's ashram as a fellow student of Brihaspati but he realized that Angiras paid more attention to his own son than him. Feeling disappointed and insulted, Shukracharya returned to his father's ashram. He later became the guru of asuras while Brihaspati became the guru of the devas.

The war between the devas and the asuras had been ongoing for ages. At one point during the war, the king of the asuras, Vrishaparva, came to Shukracharya and said, 'The devas are overpowering us. Please protect us.' Shukracharya consoled him and said, 'Don't worry. I will meditate and pray to Lord Shiva and earn a vidya (boon) from him which would save you.' Saying this, Shukracharya sat down in a meditation of a thousand years. He prayed to Lord Shiva and after the passage of thousand years, Shiva blessed him with the knowledge of mrit sanjeevani. As the name suggests in Sanskrit, sanjeevani is a herb which when consumed gives a new lease of life. Now, no matter how many asuras Indra, the king of Devlok, killed, Guru Shukracharya would make every dead asura come alive, leaving the devas helpless.

Devlok was in turmoil and Indra was deeply worried; mrit sanjeevani was making the asuras invincible and a strategy was now needed if Devlok was to remain unconquered. One day, Indra summoned Brihaspati and his son Kacha. Indra instructed Kacha to get the knowledge of sanjeevani from Guru Shukracharya; it was imperative now to secure that secret to beat the asuras in their own game. Like every ruler who has an intelligence service with the best of his spies working for him, Indra appointed Kacha as his spy. But they both knew that he would never be able to take this secret out from Shukracharya without a disuise; so Kacha decided to go to him as his student in Danavlok. Kacha was selected for this mission because he was intelligent, courageous, young and cautious.

Kacha left for Shonitpur where Shukracharya's ashram was. Shonitpur was the centre of education for the asuras. As a disciple of Shukracharya, Kacha had to go and live in the enemy town. Before leaving, the devas warned him that his life would always be in peril and that he would have to depend on his own ability to survive there as nobody could help him there. Chanakya too mentions this in Arthashastra where he states that a spy should be paid a salary but will have no protection in the enemy territory; they are their own saviours. Similarly, Kacha was on his own in Shukracharya's Danavlok.

Meanwhile, as Kacha approached his destination, he wondered: *What was the difference between devas and asuras? Was it a difference in looks, difference in thoughts or difference in power? Maybe none of these. The difference was in the purpose. The asuras could go to any extent to meet their goal but not the devas. The universe had created devas for selfless karma. To maintain the equilibrium between the devas and asuras, securing the knowledge of mrit sanjeevani from Shukracharya was the only option.*

Kacha went to Shukracharya's ashram and after introducing himself, requested him to consider him as his disciple. Kacha was so focused on his mission that he failed to notice the presence of Devyani, Shukracharya's daughter. Little did he know that one day it would be Devyani who would help him in reaching his goal. Seeing his ashram brother's son standing in front of him, Guru Shukracharya asked Kacha why he wanted to seek his education specifically from him. In reply, Kacha told him that that there was no greater guru than him in the entire universe. Shukracharya was happy with his answer and agreed to take him as his student. But the asuras objected to his decision. They said they would not let Kacha live in Danavlok as he was the son of the enemy. But Guru Shukracharya snubbed them and said that only he could take the decision on whom he wanted to teach, and not the asuras. He allowed Kacha to live in the ashram, but with a warning that his safety was only guaranteed as long as he stayed inside the premises of the ashram.

It is said that when Kacha got the permission for living in the ashram, he requested Shukracharya that he wished to follow celibacy for a thousand years and spend that time serving him and acquiring whatever knowledge he would give him.

Soon Guru Shukracharya began Kacha's education. He taught him about everything from the mysteries hidden in nature to the minute differences of the environment. A major part of the initial education was the role of every living and non-living thing in this universe and its relation to the balance of life. Ayurveda was also an integral part of Kacha's education. But he had just one question echoing through his mind: after all, what was the knowledge of mrit sanjeevani. Was it a herb, a chant or a magical ritual? It was a riddle, and it was important for him to find an answer to it. He kept his senses on high alert for he never knew when Guru Shukracharya might mention something about sanjeevani vidya. But very soon Kacha realized that it was not possible to get the information on sanjeevani so easily as it was a guarded secret.

Kacha was very patient as he knew that patience was the key to attaining this knowledge. In those times, it was the guru who used to decide when to impart any particular knowledge to his pupils. The rules and the discipline in the ashram were so strict that Kacha wouldn't know dawn from dusk. His education was in progress and Kacha was learning in earnest.

Meanwhile, Kacha was so engrossed in his lessons that he did not even notice Devyani's growing affection for him. When Kacha would be with the guru, Devyani used to be busy looking after the ashram. And whenever he used to study on his own, she would always be around to take care of him and his everyday needs. Though she never tried to distract him from his concentration or his vow of celibacy, she had fallen in love with him.

Whenever the guru was busy in his other errands, Kacha would utilize that time talking to Devyani. He found her to be a very innocent girl who would always talk openly about her thoughts. It appeared that in the ashram surrounded by the asuras, she was looking for a friend. Kacha too liked spending time with her; those were the only moments his mind would ever get diverted from his aim. Gradually, Kacha understood that Devyani was getting attracted to him and it was no longer one-sided, he realized.

In the tradition of gurukul, the student used to go and live with the guru in his ashram along with his family. The guru's wife was called 'guru mata', and it was a part of the pupil's duty and education to run domestic errands for the guru and the guru mata. Chores would include getting things for the household, making medicines, shepherding the cows, helping in cleaning, collecting firewood, etc. This is what Kacha also did at Shukracharya's ashram. He started helping out Devyani in the daily chores of the ashram. In the comfort of the ashram and in the presence of Devyani, he started forgetting that the asuras were waiting for him to leave the security of the ashram.

One day he stepped out into the forest with the cattle of his guru. Oblivious to his surroundings, Kacha was immersed in a series of thoughts. He wondered if Guru Shukracharya realized his purpose of coming to Danavlok and if Devyani was actually attracted to him. Lost in his thoughts, he lost track of time; the twilight of the arriving dusk was blurring his mission. Suddenly, he saw death surrounding him in the form of asuras who had finally caught up with him in the forest. He felt that his end had come. But more than being afraid of death, he was disappointed with himself that he had failed in completing the task entrusted upon him by his father and Indra.

Meanwhile, at the ashram, Devyani was getting worried because Kacha had not returned from the forest. She started fearing for his safety. When she saw the cattle returning at the end of the day without Kacha, her worst fear was proven true and she hastily went to her father to inform him about Kacha's absence. But it was too late by then; Guru Shukracharya through his power realized that Kacha had been killed. But his daughter was distressed beyond control. She was so tormented that even stones would have melted watching her tears and Guru Shukracharya was her father who loved her immensely. He decided to use mrit sanjeevani to revive Kacha from the dead. This was the knowledge for which Kacha had come to Danavlok but since he was no longer alive, he could not see it being used.

Meanwhile, the asuras had killed Kacha and had immersed his dead body in a river but the sanjeevani vidya worked its magic. Soon Kacha was not only made alive but was also re-established inside the ashram. On coming back to life, Kacha himself wondered if he was for real. From that moment on, he forever remained indebted to Devyani's love.

According to Mihir Bhutia, when Devyani tells her father to bring Kacha back to life, he informs her that these worshippers of Lord Shiva, meaning the asuras, were far removed from the customs of Brahmins. This hints at the fact that the relationship between the asuras and Shukracharya was a very delicate one. Shukracharya needed the asuras as much as they needed him; yet they did not trust each other completely.

Kacha had been brought up in Devlok on the concept that beauty of looks, thoughts and feelings were limited to either the land of devas or the land of humans. Danavlok, on the other hand, was inhabited by vices like delinquency, greed and general wrongdoings. But when he looked at Devyani he felt otherwise. He wondered how Devyani was so beautiful and intelligent when she was from Danavlok and, more importantly, was the daughter of the guru of asuras himself. The feeling which was germinating within her heart for Kacha was considered to be the most sacred of all the three worlds—the feeling of love.

Kacha and Devyani were both young and must have been around the same age. According to the Mahabharata, they both used to sing and dance during their leisure hours. They used to meet each other which was not against the rules of the ashram. Devyani's innocent love gradually started captivating Kacha. At times, he wanted to forget everything and stay put in his guru's ashram forever. His selfish desire was making his aim fuzzy and this started diminishing

KACHA

the boundary between the devas and the asuras in his mind. However, soon good sense prevailed over Kacha, and he realized that he had come to the Danavlok with a different goal and he had to complete it as early as possible. Time was passing by, and his education was advancing well. But he still didn't know how he could get hold of the knowledge of sanjeevani. And then one day, the much awaited opportunity arrived. A demon was brought dead to the ashram. Guru Shukracharya had to perform his vidya again to revive him; he thought that Kacha was engrossed in meditation during the act but Kacha was meditating only for the knowledge of sanjeevani.

This was the first time Kacha witnessed his guru practise the art of sanjeevani. He wondered if it was judicious to bring anybody back to life without giving it a second thought. Why were only the asuras benefitting from this privilege? It was true that Kacha himself was awarded his life back owing to his guru's love for his daughter, but shouldn't people of all the three worlds be entitled to this knowledge's benefit? He decided that he would directly ask his guru to teach him this ritual. But before he could do so, once again the asuras were a step ahead of him and killed him.

Guru Shukracharya kept his knowledge completely

hidden from everyone for five hundred years. Kacha was believed to have made several attempts to learn the art of sanjeevani. At times when Shukracharya was bringing a demon back to life, Kacha tried to observe him from hiding; at others times, when Shukracharya was practising his rituals, Kacha tried to eavesdrop. And in this constant effort, Kacha got killed time and again by the demons—once even being fed to the dogs. That time Kacha thought that was the end of his life but Guru Shukracharya once again began the ritual to bring him back to life. Perhaps he thought that Kacha had come to attain the wisdom of sanjeevani or maybe his decision was based on his love for his daughter. Kacha did not know the real reason—which was Devyani's love for him—at that time but importantly once again he returned to life and to the materialistic world.

After sometime, it seemed that Kacha knew that he would die and Devyani would help him get back to life every time; this would keep happening and maybe sometime during this whole process he would get the secret of sanjeevani. One day Kacha strategized to go to the jungle again where the demons were waiting to kill him. Kacha told Devyani that he was going to get some rare flowers for her so that she could adorn her hair with these. Devyani was not happy with the idea and she tried to dissuade him but Kacha insisted. And despite knowing that his security was ensured only till the precincts of the ashram, he stepped out. Devyani's love had become Kacha's shield.

This time, Kacha invited the demons upon himself. He wanted them to come and attack him. Once again, the land of the demons was waiting to get soaked in his blood. But this time, merely killing Kacha was not the end to the demons' heinous plan; it was just the beginning. For a very long time they had suspected that Kacha sought the mrit sanjeevani knowledge and though they killed him over and over again, it was Guru Shukracharya who ensured that the death was never final. This time they devised a way to make the death irretrievable. They burnt his dead body so that there would be no trace of his remains. But they made a mistake. They mixed Kacha's ashes in an alcohol pot and served it to Guru Shukracharya. Oblivious to the demons' odious act, Guru Shukracharya drank the alcohol offered to him. Little did he know that he was actually drinking his own disciple!

Shukracharya was a Brahmin and a sage. He was not a cannibal like the demons he was surrounded with. The atrocious act which the demons did was against the dignity of their guru. It conveyed an act of distrust against their guru; they were sceptical of Guru Shukracharya being able to guard the secrecy of the sanjeevani vidya and this was a ploy to seal Kacha's fate forever.

When Kacha did not return for a long time, Devyani got worried and went to the jungle looking for him. She found a flower dripping with blood, and knew that her worst fears had come true again. By the time she sought her father out for help, it was too late—the pot of alcohol was empty.

Guru Shukracharya once again resolved to use the sanjeevani vidya but this time it was a hard task. When he finally made contact with Kacha, he found him in his own stomach. He understood that this time the demons had played a trick which was very difficult to match; they had ensured that Kacha would not come out alive so easily.

Shukracharya was left in turmoil. Either he would have to die or digest Kacha. There was no other way out. He was aware of Devyani's love for Kacha and he loved his daughter too. He told Devyani that Kacha was in his stomach and if he tried to bring him back to life, Kacha would appear by slitting open his stomach which would lead to his own death. Devyani clearly stated to her father that she could neither live without him nor without Kacha. So it was important to her that they both should be alive. There was only way out now—that Kacha who was in Shukracharya's stomach was taught the ritual of sanjeevani and when Shukracharya would die in the process, Kacha in turn would bring him back to life. The tables were now turned on the demons. It was because of their abominable act that Guru Shukracharya was left with no choice but to impart the knowledge of sanjeevani to Kacha.

Guru Shukracharya informed Kacha about what he was going to do. Kacha agreed; he was a man of his words. He considered it a privilege to bring back his guru with the use of sanjeevani. Shukracharya did not explicitly state that Kacha should bring him back to life but the purpose of his teaching him the ritual of mrit sanjeevani was supposed to do that. But both Kacha and Shukracharya were men of high morals. Shukracharya only said to Kacha, 'Son, do what is right.' So when Kacha came out of his stomach, he also did what the right thing was to do at that time. He performed mrit sanjeevani art for the first time on his guru. Had he wanted he could have left him dead which would have been a deadly blow to the asuras, and the gods would have always won. But he did not do so.

As soon as Shukracharya came back to life and

opened his eyes, Kacha realized that his mission was now complete, and so was his education. The time had come for him to leave.

The seventy-seventh chapter of the Mahabharata mentions that when Kacha planned to leave for Devlok, Devyani professed her love for him and beseeched that she could not live without him. She asked him to marry her and make him his wife. Kacha however said that it was no longer possible for them to marry as he was reborn from her father, and they were now effectively brother and sister.

It is also considered a possibility that Kacha was trying to escape from Devyani because his plan was something else; he was a man who was on a mission. After religiously trying for five hundred years, he had finally secured the knowledge of mrit sanjeevani and he had to give it to the devas. It did not take long for Devyani to understand that Kacha had used her to gain the knowledge of sanjeevani. Though it was also the truth Kacha was only doing his duty.

It is common logic that only such a man should be appointed a spy whose loyalty is undisputed. When Indra sent Kacha for this job he had trusted his loyalty completely and never for a moment did Kacha compromise on his integrity. Kacha and Devyani were both young and he might have fallen in love with her, but Kacha never made any promises that he could not fulfil. Neither did he ever think that he would get married to Devyani and stay back.

Shukracharya was distressed to see his daughter in such pain but he knew Kacha was not in the wrong. His aim was the knowledge of sanjeevani. It was unfortunate that the path to it passed through the tears of Devyani. Shukracharya was considered great because he did not carry any enmity towards Kacha and did not feel that if Kacha had taken something from him he should reciprocate with retaliation. Charity is without expectations of any return. Shukracharya hid the wisdom of mrit sanjeevani for as long as possible but when it was necessary to give it away, he gave it away.

But Devyani could not control her feelings anymore and she cursed Kacha that he would never be able to make use of the knowledge of sanjeevani. Kacha knew he had hurt her immensely; so he did not get angry. He politely told her that in that case he would teach it to somebody else.

Leaving his guru and Devyani behind, Kacha made his way back to Devlok. He wondered if the universe knew that he would have to play with Devyani's emotions to attain his goal. His father had told him that it was important to get mrit sanjeevani to maintain equilibrium in the universe. Devas, asuras and sanjeevani had a promising role to play in the years to come; everybody had a role to perform, even if it was, sometimes, at the cost of a personal loss. To attain a bigger good, Kacha had taken advantage of Devyani's emotions. He felt sorry about it. But when it is about a larger good, a person may have to take it upon himself to do small wrongs for a bigger right.

Kacha wondered how the world would remember him in the times to come: a failed lover who gave up on his feelings owing to his duties or as the first spy ever to find out the wisdom of mrit sanjeevani?

Kacha was perhaps the first ever spy who went inside the enemy territory with a proper planning. That way he can be called the first spy of India.

EXPERTS

Dr Madhuri Subodh is a reader in the Hindi Department of Lady Shri Ram College, New Delhi. She specializes in Hindi literature.

Mihir Bhuta is a writer with a special interest in mythology related to the Mahabharata.

2
Jeev Siddhi

Chanakya's Spy
(320–283 BC)

When the vast Nanda empire, ruled by a selfish and hedonistic king, was defeated and slain by Chandragupta Maurya, it was drawn into the Aryavarta nation and Maurya was crowned the king. Yet, danger lurked over the young king in the form of Amatya Rakshasa, the Nanda empire's faithful minister who was out to avenge his slain master. With the arrival of Rakshasa in the picture, Chanakya's unmatched brilliance and stratagem stood to be foiled by the one man in the land who was an intellectual equal to him. Chankaya decided to deploy a spy into Rakshasa's camp, not to destroy the devious

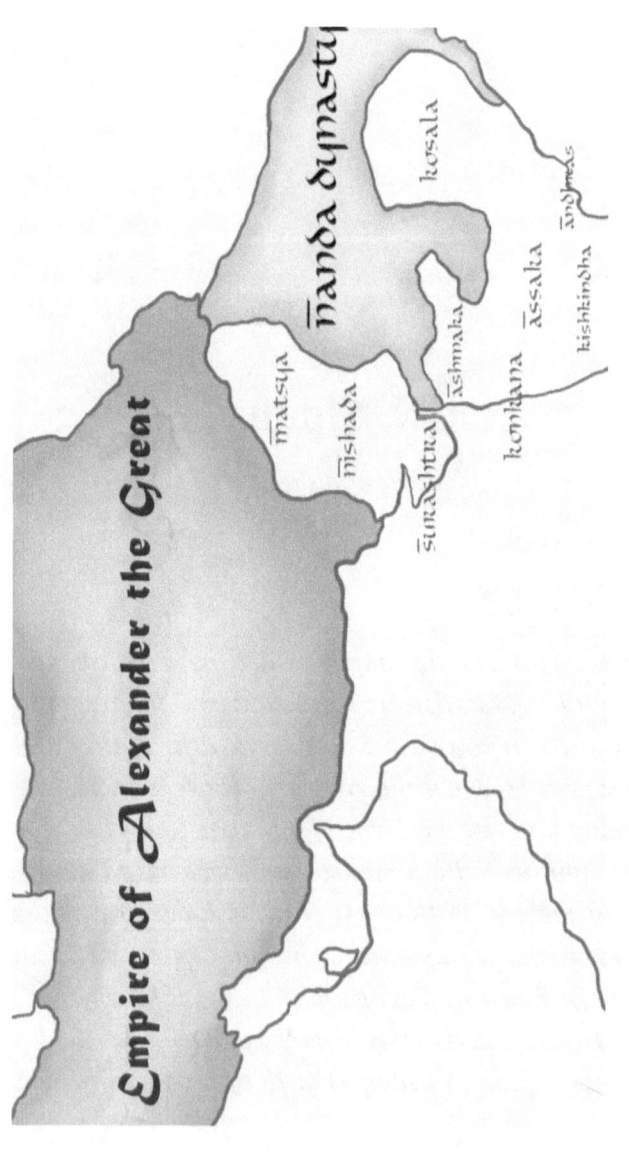

Map depicting the Nanda dynasty and the empire of Alexander

minister but to win him over. He sent forward his best man, Jeev Siddhi, disguised as a Jain monk. Trained by one of the greatest spymasters the world has ever known, Jeev Siddhi entered the innermost circles of Rakshasa's court, attempting to turn an enemy of the state into one of its most powerful ministers.

In the third century BC, Aryavarta was divided into sixteen mahajanapads (major parts). When Alexander started on his campaign of invading India approximately in the year 326 BC, he came close to achieving that but did not actually attack the country and returned from its boundary. Although nothing happened, there was one person who was keeping a keen eye on all these activities—Chanakya (also known as Kautilya and Vishnugupta). He understood that Bharat, which was divided into sixteen parts, could never fight against such a huge unanimous attack. They stood absolutely no chance against such a major foreign invasion. This marked the start of his dream of a single unified country—Bharat—which would be ruled by one king. For this, he first got in touch with King Nanda of Magadha, who was also called Dhana Nanda, and consulted him with his plans but because of the difference of opinion King Nanda did not oblige Chanakya further.

Nanda was considered a weak king; he was also malicious, cruel and was a debauch, with a penchant for dance, music and courtesans. He was not an able administrator and barely took interest in state affairs. When Chanakya penned Arthashastra, which is a treatise about his political views, he wrote about how an ideal kingdom should be: if there is a kingdom, its king should be a 'vijigishu' (desirous for or would be world conqueror). In ancient India, a king was considered a vijigishu if he aimed to win territories in all four directions. When such a king marked his victory in all directions, then a vijigishu became a chakravartin (an ideal universal ruler).

King Nanda in his pleasures

Chanakya's knowledge was not just limited to religious texts; he was also appreciated for his cognizance of politics and economics. He was also the royal advisor to Chandragupta Maurya. That was why he chose Chandragupta, his king, for the formation of a united Aryavarta.

Although Chandragupta was Nanda's son, his mother belonged to a lower caste and so he was not brought up in the royal household. As per legend, one evening in Magadha, young Chandragupta was playing with some children. There was a mound of mud on which he was sitting. Following some dispute, the children came to him and asked him to solve the matter with his able judgement. Young Chandragupta gave a brilliant solution to settle the whole issue. The children went away satisfied. Chanakya was standing afar watching this little boy and noticed this incident. He felt that the boy had something special in him. He took the child from his mother and began his education. He was sure that the child was the ideal person to carry forward his views and thus began the process of influencing the child with his dream. Enough time had elapsed since the threat of Alexander and now Chandragupta had grown up. As King Nanda had not paid any attention to Chanakya's views, he decided that Chandragupta must sit on the throne of Magadha.

Chandragupta was a brave young man. He was not just physically powerful but was also polite and obedient and respected Chanakya for his schemes and ideologies. He was competent enough to imbibe and work towards the achievement of Chanakya's goal.

Meanwhile, Chankaya wanted his dream of Aryavarta to be realized as early as possible. Owing to Chanakya's tactics, Chandragupta was installed on the royal throne, but he was not yet completely safe. His goal, though taking a gradual shape, was yet incomplete. As Chandragupta was an illegitimate heir of the Nanda clan, Chanakya knew that he was not yet safe on the throne. A major reason for that was Rakshasa, who was Nanda's chief minister, and was running Magadha on behalf of his king. A skilled administrator, Chanakya did not want him dead but wanted to win him over. But Rakshasa was a staunch loyalist. He could not shift his loyalties from one king to another. With the death of King Nanda, his reign was over and obviously Rakshasa lost his ministership. However, he could not bear the sight of anyone other than a legitimate heir of the Nanda clan sitting on the throne. He now took it upon himself, as his dharma, to avenge the death of his master by killing Chandragupta who had planned and executed the murder of Nanda. This feeling of revenge proved Rakshasa's loyalty and love for his master. He was as devoted to the Nanda dynasty, particularly King Nanda, as Chanakya was devoted to Chandragupta. Though they were enemies, yet their concern regarding the safety and well-being of their respective kings were almost similar.

Rakshasa's actual name was probably Katyayan, and Rakshasa was the title he had got for his strength, skill and valour. Rakshasa was no less than Chanakya by any means; they were both ministers to their respective kings. Also, both were strategists of the highest acumen, were thorough in diplomatic interactions, were learned scholars and, most importantly, were idealists. Time had now come to move from disorganization to organization, to challenge the destiny, to get the qualified his rightful position and to establish Aryavarta. It was at this juncture that Jeev Siddhi was deployed in a new mission.

Jeev Siddhi was an ardent follower of Chanakya, his guru. If he had become famous for his knowledge, it was because of Guru Chanakya. He could bow his head only to his God or his guru. It was a matter of great pride for him to be a part of any of Chanakya's scheme. But when Chanakya instructed him to infiltrate Rakshasa's camp, he realized that this time the mission was not an easy one. This was the time when Rakshasa was hiding at a secret place outside Magadha and was planning to kill Chandragupta. Jeev Siddhi, however, accepted the task.

With a new disguise also came a new name—Jeev Siddhi.

Arthashastra tells us as to how spies should disguise themselves when on a mission; it even recommends training them for this. The disguises can vary from a gemstone merchant, a craftsman, a cook, a snake charmer or a prostitute when it is a woman. But the most important disguise that it suggests is that of a mendicant. It can be a Buddhist or a Jain monk, a hermit even, who in Sanskrit is called a parivrajak (for men) or parivrajika (for women). This garb of a mendicant is termed 'nirdosham vesham', which means a guise free of any flaw or a guise which cannot be doubted upon. A mendicant is free to go to any town, to anybody's house and meet anybody in search of alms; he/she can never be doubted. Jeev Siddhi chose to become a Jain monk and found an easy entry into the camp of Rakshasa.

Now, Jeev Siddhi had many doubts but he knew that he had to work for the ultimate goal and prove his worth to his guru. On entering the camp, his next strategy was to gain Rakshasa's trust. However, he was unaware that he was not alone on this path. Chanakya had several other spies set on the same goal.

Although Jeev Siddhi was an important spy of Chanakya, he was not the only one for the master strategist. There were two or three more like him who had covered the entire town. And to top it all, they didn't know of each other's existence. Each used to handle the single task assigned to him. Only Chanakya knew how these seemingly isolated tasks would ultimately combine in the end to complete the whole plan.

Chanakya's Arthashastra tells us that spies must learn different languages and different costumes but a special emphasis is also paid to the learning of different arts and techniques. Astrology is the most recommended among all these and has been referred as 'mahurat kabi'—someone who could read time. This art requires not just the garb of an astrologer but his knowledge too. And Jeev Siddhi was an expert in this as is evident in the story of *Mudrarakshasa* in which Jeev Siddhi is portrayed not only as a Jain hermit but also as someone expert in astrology.

Chanakya says that to win people's confidence, one cannot simply go as a common man and say he has some special knowledge; he would not be believed. To gain trust, in tandem with wearing the correct disguise, he would also have to showcase his accomplishment, which should be extraordinary. So, accordingly, Jeev Siddhi had come prepared for this.

It was a testing time for him; it was not easy to dupe Amatya Rakshasa. On being presented to him, when Jeev Siddhi said that he had astrological power, Rakshasa said he had not been surprised for a long time; so he must open his mouth only if he can give him any interesting news. Else, he should simply walk away.

Jeev Siddhi knew that it was time to play his cards as instructed by Guru Chanakya. He told Rakshasa that the seventh closed room of Nand Mahal held a secret. Years ago when a Brahmin had opposed Nanda's ways, he was murdered in that room. Chanakya had told him this secret; very few people knew about it. Amatya Rakshasa too was aware of this incident. He was surprised by this sudden piece of information and with this Jeev Siddhi gained his trust.

One day Rakshasa called Jeev Siddhi; he had a task for him. He asked Jeev Siddhi to look into his astrological charts and suggest a good day to poison Chandragupta. Without losing his composure, Jeev Siddhi looked at the charts and said that if the work was done looking into the direction of Mangal (Mars), somebody's death was assured. Then, he informed his guru about Rakshasa's plan at the earliest.

Arthashastra teaches various methods of attaining victory over the enemy. Now there was something called an indirect victory, wherein the enemy was weakened or finished off gradually and discreetly. This involved the use of medicines and mantras (chants), which find a special mention in Arthashastra. Interestingly, the names of some such medicines and poisons which are mentioned in Arthashastra also find a mention in *Sushruta Samhita*, which was the book of medicine of that time. This leads us to believe that Chanakya's suggestions on killing opponents were based on science.

Rakshasa had a web of spies in Magadha. One of them was Abhaydutt, and his role came under the category of 'rasad'. Arthashastra gives us an insight into the categorization of spies: sapri, teekshn, rasad and bhikshuki. Rasad means 'rasam dadati saharasda', a translation of which would mean someone who gives the juice. Ras or juice here can mean two things: medicine or poison. This means that a medicine doctor or rasad must have the knowledge of poison along with medicine. He should also know how to mix poison in medicine. This was why Abhaydutt, who was a great doctor, was chosen by Rakshasa for the task of killing Chandragupta by poisoning him. But when Abhaydutt offered a bowl of medicine to Chandragupta, Chanakya made him drink it instead. The spy–vaidya died soon after, proving Chanakya's suspicion right. According to Arthashastra and even old political science, before giving any medicine to the king, the vaidya or doctor must first taste the medicine himself to check it for poison.

Before Chandragupta had attacked Magadha, to gain more power, he had formed an alliance with King Parvatak. King Parvatak had a huge mountainous empire and was a powerful king, which led to Chanakya suggesting a treaty between the two kingdoms. Under the treaty, it was agreed that the kingdom of Magadha would be divided equally between Chandragupta and Parvatak. But once Magadha was acquired, Chanakya was not keen anymore on a division of Chandragupta's empire. That's when Rakshasa unknowingly sent an opportunity in Chanakya's way, when he used a vishkanya to kill Chandragupta.

The concept of a vishkanya is very intriguing, so much so, that it seems almost mythical. Although this concept gets a mention in Arthashastra, it's rarely present in any other historical text. Interestingly though it is present in the *Sushruta Samhita*, which indicates that this concept can have some connection with herbal medicine science practised during that time. It is believed that a vishkanya was a girl who was fed small quantities of poison regularly till her whole body became poisonous. Right from her skin, her breath and even her eyes became so lethal that anyone coming in contact with her would die. Another more believable version of the myth of vishkanya is that the woman would put poison cream on her body, including her private parts. Then she would go to the enemy and when she had established a relationship with him, he would die coming in contact with the lethal cream.

In *Mudrarakshasa*, a vishkanya is compared to that of Indra's power (boon) which can be used only once. When she would kill a king with her poison, it is evident that she too would be killed by his people, which meant that she could also be used only once.

Jeev Siddhi knew that there was going to be another attack after the failed attempt of the Abhaydutt incident. Time was precious, and there were strong chances of things going wrong. He knew that the poison maiden was about to leave to kill Chandragupta. There were great chances that this time Rakshasa's strategy would work. This was vital information, and he had to let his guru know; the difficulty lay in letting Chanakya know this in time. Jeev Siddhi had no other way than to take things head on, even at the cost of his own security. He attempted to go himself.

While he was trying to go unnoticed, a soldier saw him. At first afraid that he was caught, he soon figured that the soldier who was wearing a Nanda soldier's uniform, was actually a spy Chanakya had sent to help Jeev Siddhi deliver messages. Jeev Siddhi handed over the piece of information to him and asked him to get it to his guru at the earliest.

On the same day, King Parvatak was also there at the court of Chandragupta. At one point of time though he had played a vital role in securing Magadha, he was now an impediment to the bigger plans of Aryavarta. So Chanakya, who read Jeev Siddhi's secret message, gifted the poison maiden to Parvatak. Parvatak was elated to receive such a beautiful woman and was pleased that he got priority over Chandragupta for this beautiful gift. He considered it his honour.

With this trick, Chanakya killed more than one bird with a single arrow. First, he ensured Chandragupta's safety and diverted the danger away from him. Second,

Parvatak, who was hindering the dream of a united state, got killed without much effort. Third, Chanakya spread the rumour that Rakshasa had murdered Parvatak. This induced the citizens into hating Rakshasa. With one stroke, Chanakya achieved three results.

Meanwhile, Jeev Siddhi knew that though Rakshasa's plan had backfired and he was disappointed, he hadn't given up. He was sure to make another attempt on Chandragupta's life.

Once, after victory in a battle, when Chandragupta was supposed to enter the capital city of Pataliputra, the toran (gateway) to the main entrance was made weak by Rakshasa's spy. The plan was that when Chandragupta with his entourage would enter the city, it would fall on him, leading to his death. Jeev Siddhi, who was then keeping a close eye on Rakshasa and his associates, was shocked when he came to know of Rakshasa's new plan. It was a planned accident which was going to take place in front of the whole city, a spectacle of death. Jeev Siddhi informed Chanakya on time and the latter immediately came up with a counter plan. Instead of Chandragupta, he made another prince dress up as the king and made him sit on an elephant and enter first.

Fortunately, when the toran fell, the prince had a lucky escape and the broken toran fell on the mahot. The elephant rider, who was actually Rakshasa's man, died instantly.

Rakshasa's plans had failed one after the other, and he was losing his patience. He decided to declare war and asked Jeev Siddhi to look for an auspicious date. Jeev Siddhi could no longer resist himself and said that although the planets were aligned it was against Rakshasa's interest. He suggested that perhaps he should enter into a treaty with the Maurya kingdom. He then looked at the sky outside and pointing to the full moon which had risen, he said that this was further proof that Chandragupta was ready to rule. So Rakshasa's best bet would be to declare truce with Chanakya.

Rakshasa was a bit perplexed hearing this suggestion. The future of Bharat depended on his decision. Had he been insistent on removing Chandragupta, sooner or later he would have achieved that goal and Bharat would have lost the Maurya dynasty even before its inception. That moment was crucial for the country, and for Chanakya to wait and for Jeev Siddhi to prove himself. It was also a moment for Rakshasa where he had to rise above his personal choices and choose a side.

Finally, Rakshasa agreed to Jeev Siddhi's counsel;

Chanakya offered the post of Chandragupta's amatya (minister) to him. He told him that his intelligence and his capabilities should be of use to the Aryavarta and to Chandragupta; so it would be in everybody's interest to accept the post. Rakshasa too gratefully accepted Chankaya's proposal.

Jeev Siddhi too revealed to him his true allegiance.

Like Chanakya, Rakshasa too was loyal to his lord and both were great strategists. Rakshasa noticed these qualities of Chanakya and must have felt that it was not so bad to bow his head to the wishes of a man who was so much like himself. Also, he had realized that Chanakya's fight and efforts were not for any personal gain but for a larger goal, for a stronger future and for an ideal principle. He understood that Chankaya did all of these to establish the root of a perfect kingdom.

Despite holding such a powerful position, Chanakya had played his cards to win over Rakshasa and not just to eradicate him. As soon as the latter accepted the position offered, Chanakya left the kingdom for the jungles. According to the prevalent tradition of the Hindu caste system, it was considered the duty of a Brahmin to learn and impart knowledge. Therefore, when Chanakya provided an able minister to Chandragupta, he realized that his dream was already underway and he could leave the kingdom in safe hands. In the jungle, he continued with his learning and authored the seminal work Arthashastra which till date serves as a guideline for many.

Jeev Siddhi too realized that the objective of his teacher was achieved. When Chanakya left, never once looking back, Jeev Siddhi walked after him, following his footsteps, bowing to his ideologies. The biggest lesson he could learn from his guru was how to remove oneself from the mainstream and move towards self-development.

If we try to decipher all the incidents which took place under Chanakya's guidance, then it would not be correct to limit our understanding to just his politics. A farsighted man like Chanakya was fighting for a principle. He was not eying just a kingdom. Rather, he wanted to take the society forward, from maladministration to good governance and perfection.

In Sanskrit drama, it is a practice to begin any play with a short poem, usually praising the deities. What is interesting is that in the play *Mudrarakshasa*, Vishakhdutt, its creator, praises Chanakya for his immense intelligence. He says that we must bow to this man who defeated an army with his sharp mind. And not just any army but the army of the Nandas which was deemed so powerful that by just listening to their victory stories Alexander had refrained from attacking India. Chanakya defeated such an army with his brilliant political acumen and clever strategies but he needed an able man to execute such an intricate plan. It was a spy like Jeev Siddhi who helped his master in his mission.

EXPERTS

Dr Asawari Bapat is a visiting lecturer at the University of Mumbai. Dr Bapat specializes in Sanskrit literature and teaches the *Mudrarakshasa* and Arthashastra.

Dr Shonaleeka Kaul is a cultural historian and is the author of *Imagining the Urban: Sanskrit and the City in Early India*. Dr Kaul teaches at the University of Delhi and her area of specialization is Sanskrit texts such as the *Mudrarakshasa*.

3
Chand Bardai
The Poet Spy
(1148–91)

A court poet, a jester and a master of disguises, Chand Bardai served under Prithviraj Chauhan, the king of the Hindu Chauhan dynasty that ruled over Ajmer (Rajasthan) and Delhi. Faithful to his master, Bardai was involved in helping Chauhan's beloved Sanyukta escape from Kannauj on the day of her swayamvar. When Prithviraj was defeated by Ghori in the second battle of Tarain and taken as a prisoner, Bardai followed Chauhan as a fakir and won favour with Ghori. He is said to have found Prithviraj Chauhan in the prison cell of Ghazni, blinded and in chains. Together with

CHAND BARDAI

his master, Bardai plotted a way to seek revenge from the cruel Ghori. Through a simple couplet that only Bardai and Chauhan could follow, the king and his poet managed to kill Ghori in his very own court, avenging the humiliation of the Rajput king. While Bardai and Prithviraj killed themselves right after, their story lives on through Prithviraj Raso, *written in praise of Prithviraj and completed by Bardai's son, Jalhan, and the court poets to come.*

Chand Bardai was the court poet of Prithviraj Chauhan. His composition *Prithviraj Raso*, on the life of Prithviraj, is considered the first Hindi epic and is a very popular text. Bardai was a confidante, friend and adviser to Prithviraj and was a valued courtier; thus, he got an opportunity to have a closer look into Prithviraj's life and other indulgencies which he closely documented in this very beautiful composition.

Prithviraj and Bardai were born on the same date and even at the same place. Possibly, since then the strings of their lives had intertwined forever. Bardai had known Prithviraj very closely since they were children. On growing up, his only aim was to ensure that the story of a brave man like Prithviraj Chauhan should not be lost to the future generations. That was the driving inspiration for the penning of *Prithviraj Raso* which became the most important objective of his life. Apart from writing, he had another crucial role to execute—he was a spy to Prithviraj. He had to disguise himself frequently and tour through Prithviraj's reign to check the kingdom's borders and also the well-being of their citizens.

In the 12th century, northern India had two major empires. One was the Chauhan empire with Delhi and Ajmer as its two important cities. The second was the kingdom of Kannauj, ruled by the Gahadavala clan. King Jaichand was the ruler of Kannauj, and his contemporary, Prithviraj Chauhan ruled from Delhi. They were both strategically and economically capable states, and their citizens were happy under their rule. Despite this, they both wanted to expand their empires which became a reason of constant tension and animosity between them. To add to it, there were some personal strains as well.

Tales of Prithviraj's qualities and his unparalleled valour had reached Sanyukta, the beautiful and young daughter of Jaichand. There was a daasi (maid) in the palace, named Madna, who used to keep company to the royal princess. Madna herself was very much in awe

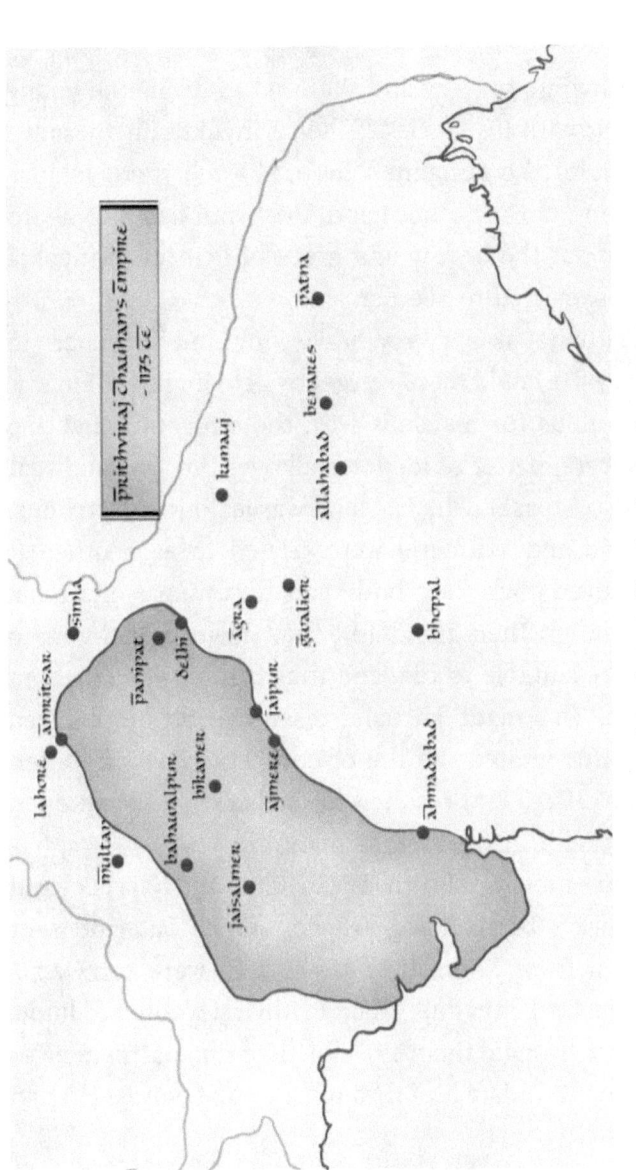

Map of Prithviraj Chauhan's empire

of Prithviraj's bravery and she used to regale the young princess with his stories. When Sanyukta finally saw a portrait of the acclaimed hero, she fell more in love with him. On the other hand, Prithviraj had also heard a lot about the beauty and grace of Princess Sanyukta and he yearned to see her.

Prithviraj was a very brave king and an expert in archery. He could hit his target by listening to it. He was also famous for his skills with the sword; his fighting skills were matter of folklores all over the land and that was also a reason why Jaichand was jealous and anxious. Jaichand and Prithviraj were related to each other. It is believed that they both had a common maternal grandfather. Their grandfather had deemed Prithviraj to be more suitable to rule and thus had left his kingdom to him. This made Jaichand resentful and he objected to it. This ignited the fire of competitiveness between the two kings and resulted in Jaichand declaring open enmity with Prithviraj Chauhan.

Since then Raja Prithviraj Chauhan and Raja Jaichand had always been at loggerheads. Once Jaichand sent his men from Kannauj to Delhi who were carrying a message for Prithviraj. When Prithviraj wanted to know what had brought them to Delhi, the principal messenger tried to intimidate him through a web of words. He told

Prithviraj that Delhi was going to witness a storm soon, a storm which could not be stopped by any wall. It was strange that the messengers from Kannauj had come so far to provide Prithviraj with a weather update. Kannauj was boiling in its envy against Delhi and that message was just a game of words but the actual meaning behind the massage was crystal clear to Prithviraj; the king of Kannauj had sent him an open challenge. But Raja Prithviraj was no less. He was a courageous king. He would have never accepted subjugation under any other king. It was against kingship protocol to harm a messenger, which was why the messengers from Kannauj were allowed to leave Delhi safely. But before that, Prithviraj gave them a befitting reply in his own style. He said that if Jaichand wanted to rule over Delhi, he would have to meet him in the battleground, instead of hiding behind a messenger.

Raja Jaichand had played the dice first and Raja Prithviraj had accepted his challenge. It was yet to be seen who would roll the dice next.

Meanwhile, Chand Bardai was a close confidante to Prithviraj. Bardai had been constantly present to help his friend in his every endeavour. He had played a crucial role in bringing all of Prithviraj Chauhan's love affairs into reality; this finds a mention in *Prithviraj Raso* which is replete with his heroic and love tales. The sound of Prithviraj's sword clashing in the battle as well as the delicate sound of anklets that could be heard in his fort are documented in nuanced details in *Prithviraj Raso*.

The love story blossoming between Prithviraj and Sanyukta had become an extremely beautiful and important part of Bardai's life. Prithviraj was an expert at expressing his feelings but he could not write; so the onus of penning his feelings into words was on Bardai. He used to enjoy doing it as much as writing *Raso*. Those letters became a part of *Raso* later. Deeply in love with each other, Prithviraj and Sanyukta could not meet each other, but with the help of her dear parrot, they could exchange letters which added further passion to their story.

Unaware of the enmity between Jaichand and Prithviraj, Sanyukta used to desperately wait for Prithviraj's letters. Colour would rush to her face when she heard the flapping of the wings of the parrot, bringing a letter for her. The way Bardai was a friend to Prithviraj, the same was with Sanyukta and that parrot. The bird was playing the role of a perfect messenger of love. But Bardai was anxious to know the result of that forbidden love, a love which surely would not be approved by Jaichand.

Oblivious to everybody in the royal household, Sanyukta was waiting with the picture of Prithviraj inked on her heart—waiting for the day when he would come to take her away from Kannauj. She had accepted him as her husband. Her love had grown so intense that Sanyukta could imagine nobody else as her husband. So despite living in the confines of the fort, she abandoned protocol and proactively informed her father that she had given her heart to Prithviraj and she would not marry anybody else. She requested him not to think of her swayamvar.

Jaichand, who disliked Prithviraj immensely, was enraged with his daughter's choice and considered it a betrayal. His wife advised him to get Sanyukta married as soon as possible and to arrange for her swayamvar, not heeding to what Sanyukta desired.

When Sanyukta was informed about the announcement of her swayamvar by her father, she was devastated. For Jaichand, Rajputana pride came before his daughter's happiness. But Sanyukta was a Rajput princess too; after the first blow, she decided to have her way and sent a letter to Prithviraj through her winged messenger. As soon as Prithviraj received her letter, he was deeply upset. In his aggrieved state, he could not decide what to do next. Bardai could not bear to see him like this.

While looking at the messenger parrot, Bardai suddenly came up with a brilliant idea. Just as the bird was both a messenger and a spy, delivering messages between two states, he too could infiltrate Jaichand's kingdom in a similar manner. He explained to Prithviraj that while Bardai could go to Kannauj as a prince attending the swayamvar, Prithviraj would accompany him as his servant.

Prithviraj was convinced that this plan would work and in turn he sent a letter for Sanyukta through the parrot that he would reach the swayamvar, whether invited by Jaichand or not, and she should not worry. Sanyukta's happiness knew no bounds when she read the letter.

The tradition of swayamvar was observed for royal princesses where they would choose a husband for their own selves. Princes and kings who were considered suitable used to be invited by the father of the princess and she was supposed to choose from the gathering.

Jaichand established a statue of Prithviraj near the gate of his palace where the swayamvar was being held.

It indicated that he had designated the king of Delhi as only a mere guard in the swayamvar and nothing else. Jaichand's only purpose here was to humiliate Raja Prithviraj in front of the others.

The swayamvar started and the princess entered the sabha after the announcement. One look at her and every single person attending the sabha agreed that the stories about her beauty and grace were not exaggerated at all. However, Sanyukta's eyes were searching for Prithviraj in that crowd. She couldn't see him anywhere but noticed his statue, placed by her father, in the corner. As if possessed, she walked past everyone to the statue of his and garlanded it. Prithviraj was hiding all this while in a corner and now he came out in front of everyone. Chaos ensued in the sabha; nobody could believe that Prithviraj himself was present there in the palace.

The statue of Prithviraj Chauhan which Jaichand had got erected to humiliate him had ironically become the reason for his own disgrace. Bardai's plan had worked successfully. People could not believe that Prithviraj Chauhan had been there in the fort for three days and nobody had any idea about it. Prithviraj managed to elope with Sanyukta on horseback. This insult to Jaichand was a preamble to an ensuing battle.

Subsequently, a battle took place to stop the eloping couple but Jaichand lost it. A victorious Prithviraj brought his bride Sanyukta to Delhi. As Chand Bardai writes, Delhi found its queen and Prithviraj achieved his victory.

Prithviraj and Sanyukta spent the first few months together in blissful happiness while they forgot that the danger had not passed yet. Although Kannauj had accepted defeat, it was not the only army which longed for the throne of Delhi. Bardai too had noticed that the political weather around was suggesting an imminent war and there was danger lurking around which could loom large any moment and this time, it might not be an easy win.

There are two specific lines about this in *Prithviraj Raso*: '*Aabaran aahuti sanjog, aabaran aahuti sanjogi, leyo putri chhal maagi*'. Translated, this means that Prithviraj Chauhan ran away with Jaichand's daughter deceitfully. However, Raja Jaichand could not forget this insult easily. Delhi and Kannauj were always inimical to each other, their rulers hovering around each other's boundaries and hatching plans to defeat the other. The elopement of Sanyukta with Prithviraj only made matters worse.

Meanwhile, Prithviraj's enemies were not limited

only to Jaichand in Kannauj in the east. It also spread in the west with the king of the region of Ghazni, in Afghanistan—Mohammad Ghori. Ghori had once tasted defeat in the hands of Prithviraj in the First Battle of Tarain in 1191 and was planning to avenge himself. After the abduction of Sanyukta, Jaichand got an opportunity to give the whole incident a political twist. To turn the opportunity in his favour, he started the preparation of an alliance with Ghori. The enmity and personal motives led to the Second Battle of Tarain in 1192.

At times, there is not one incident that marks a turning point in history; it can be a cluster of events which changes the course of a kingdom. What was to happen next was not in anybody's control. The next time Chand Bardai went to spy, the armies of Jaichand and Ghori had reached Delhi. Prithviraj had defeated both the armies individually but to fight the might of two armies together was a hard challenge even for him. Both Ghori and Jaichand were burning in the fire of revenge and had joined hands to give Prithviraj a suitable reply.

Prithviraj had fought many wars with many kings. Many of his wars were with Jaichand and as *Prithviraj Raso* suggests, he had fought as many as twelve wars with Mohammad Ghori. Though Ghori had come all the way from Ghazni, it was clear that he did not intend to rule. According to history, he had come to showcase his power to the kings of India. Invaders during that age came to India only with the single objective of looting the immense wealth of the rich northern plains. Ghori also came with the same intention—to fill up his coffers. In the First Battle of Tarain, it is said that Prithviraj had defeated Ghori in the war, and on the behest of his soldiers, had wanted to kill him. But just as his sword swung near his neck, Ghori fell on his feet and cried for mercy and Prithviraj held himself back. Chand Bardai described this act and portrayed the generosity, courageousness and forgiveness of his hero in *Prithviraj Raso*.

Prithviraj Chauhan granted Ghori his life, when he begged for it, but in the days to come, it was yet to be seen whether he had been generous or foolish.

Ghori won the Second Battle of Tarain in 1192, presumably because of Jaichand's assistance. Prithviraj had an army of elephants while Ghori had come with horse-riders. On the western gate, when the army of elephants tried to stop Ghori's soldiers, they were attacked from the rear end by Jaichand's soldiers who were also riding horses. Prithviraj's army could not defend both the gates and he was defeated; he was captured and bound in chains.

According to the tradition of the time, when a Rajput king saw a defeat approaching in a battle, he would rather die fighting in the battleground than get captured. It was either victory or death for him. The position of the queens became perilous in such a situation because they could be harmed by the victorious king. To preserve their self-respect and dignity they accepted the sati tradition. *Raso* says that after the defeat of Prithviraj Chauhan, Sanyukta, along with her companions and ladies-in-waiting, performed the jauhar, a custom of mass self-immolation, to protect their honour.

Having captured Prithviraj, Ghori took him to Ghazni. Chand Bardai, meanwhile, managed to stay at different locations in different disguises after the defeat of his king. Jaichand's spies were looking for him but he could not leave Prithviraj alone in his hour of distress. Neither his pen, nor he himself nor history was willing to accept that a king as valorous as Prithviraj should die in captivity of some other king. Before departing on his journey to be with Prithviraj, Chand Bardai handed over his creation to his son Jalhan, so that he could continue to write their story further. He now had only one aim in his life: to free Prithviraj from the jails of Ghori but for that he needed to go to Ghazni. Though the journey was not an easy one, Chand Bardai started with a firm aim in his mind and he knew that time was too short. By the time he reached Ghazni, after such a long and perilous trip, his appearance had changed considerably. The hardships he faced on the way had made his body weak; he was a different Chand Bardai altogether.

Chand Bardai, even before he made the trip, was aware that the citizens of Ghazni were very superstitious. For a state whose warriors in the First Battle of Tarain had believed elephants to be some magical creatures and had run away from it, Chand Bardai thought that the best way to earn a name for himself would be to go as a fakir who could perform magic.

To attract people's attentions, he came up with different magic shows and also used his knowledge of astrology to announce that he could hide the sun. He even used magic tricks to produce gold coins out of thin air.

When Ghori got to know of his abilities he became curious to meet the man, and Chand Bardai was presented before him. He showed him many tricks and gained his confidence. As he was an expert astrologer, he calculated the next solar eclipse and when the time came, he played the trick of making the sun disappear. People, including Ghori, were left stunned.

No doubt Ghori was an ace warrior but like his citizens he too was superstitious. When he saw the solar eclipse, he assumed that Bardai could hide the sun with his magical power and accepted that Bardai was indeed a very powerful man. He now wanted Chand Bardai to help him win in his wars. He welcomed Bardai in his court, gave him the title of a royal guest and included him in his inner circle. Thus Bardai won the king's heart and became his trusted friend.

Now that he had infiltrated Ghori's circle, Bardai started strategizing the next step. He was constantly thinking of how to find his friend and king Prithviraj who was in captivity. As a royal guest he was allowed to move around at his will but he was not allowed to meet the prisoners kept in the jail. But he was desperate to see Prithviraj and so he found a way to visit the jail. At the jail, he used to sing songs in Brij language which he knew only Prithviraj could decipher. One day, while walking through the prison, suddenly a wounded hand grabbed his leg. And that's how the loyal friend found Prithviraj in captivity in the middle of the Ghazni kingdom.

Chand Bardai had found his friend, his Prithvi. But he had never thought even in his dreams that Ghori's hatred would go to such an extent where he would torture the man so mercilessly. He was shattered witnessing the cruelty and malignancy of Ghori where even Prithviraj's eyes were gouged out in torture.

Prithviraj said to him that he did not want to run away from there. He just wanted to avenge the disgrace that had befallen him. Bardai was to help him in every way possible, and he promised him that. On hearing Ghori's soldiers approaching, Bardai quickly left from there, however, bent on a revenge plan to make Ghori pay up. He thought of ways to free his king and an idea struck him. He encouraged Ghori to arrange for an archery competition to see which of his soldiers was best with the bow.

Ghori agreed to Bardai's suggestion and the archery competition started. The latter did not purposely appreciate Ghori's best archer who obviously did not like that he could not impress Bardai. Having patiently waited for some time, finally he asked Chand Bardai what was it he wanted to see in Ghazni's best archers. It was just the question Chand Bardai was waiting for. He immediately answered, 'Raja Prithviraj Chauhan. He can hit his target with his eyes closed and just by listening to a sound. No wonder Ghori's archers did not stand a chance before him.'

Chand Bardai had already won Ghori's heart. So he did not doubt him and agreed to Prithviraj being brought to the arena.

It was Bardai's last plan in Ghori's assembly and it was a masterstroke—a plan which was first laid out in Delhi but the climax of which was unfolding in Ghazni. Ghori was unaware that while in Delhi, Bardai and Prithviraj had done a special experiment in which Bardai used to just tell him the distance of the target and keeping that in mind, Prithviraj used to correctly hit his target.

A bow and arrow was given to Prithviraj. Bardai, who was standing close to him, recited a couplet to him:

> *Chaar baans, choubis gaj,*
> *Angul ashtha pramaan,*
> *Taa oopar sultan hai,*
> *Chooke mat Chauhan.*

What it meant was this: measure four bamboos and add twenty-four yards to it. To this, add a little more distance of eight fingers and the sultan is sitting just above that. Don't miss it, Chauhan. Prithviraj smiled at Bardai and quickly changing direction, hit his target—

the neck of Mohammad Ghori.

At Ghori's death, when Prithviraj and Bardai were taken prisoners, they both killed each other with daggers because they knew what their fate would be in Ghazni. Thus, Chand Bardai saved his king from getting humiliated even further and dying a tortuous death but in the effort gave away his life too. The story of his genius planning and sacrifice became famous among his people; he was not just a loyal courtier to his king but had tried to protect the honour of his master till his last breath. He could not free him physically, but he got him released from a life of servitude to another king and in that way protected his self-respect and dignity. At one point in *Raso*, it is mentioned,

> *Ek deh utpann,*
> *Ek deh samaye krum.*

The couplet means that both Prithviraj Chauhan and Chand Bardai were born at the same time, and they died at the same time too. The story of Bardai's loyalty and their friendship has been told and retold for generations in Rajasthan.

EXPERTS

Dr Madhuri Subodh is a reader in the Hindi Department of Lady Shri Ram College, University of Delhi. She specializes in Hindi literature.

Dr Nandini Sinha Kapur is the director of the School of Inter-disciplinary and Trans-disciplinary Studies at the Indira Gandhi National Open University (IGNOU), New Delhi.

4
Bahirji Naik

*Chhatrapati Shivaji Maharaj's
Chief Intelligence Officer*
(17th century)

In a country that was ruled by the Mughals in the north and the Deccan sultanates in the south, Shivaji Maharaj Bhonsle, a jagirdar's son, began at the age of sixteen, to bring down the two hundred-year old Adil Shahi empire with a handful of soldiers. Practitioners of Ganimi Kawa or Shiva Sutra, Shivaji's army overcame its small size by fierce war strategies—taking the enemy by surprise. At the army's head was its chief intelligence officer, Bahirji Naik, a tribal warrior who was chosen by Shivaji himself to lead. Bahirji Naik, the master of disguises, has managed to silently sink into the pages of history, but traces of his genius can be seen in the way the Adil Shahi empire was brought down by three hundred odd men, how Lal Mahal was recaptured from the ruthless Aurangzeb's army and how the drying coffers of the Maratha empire was replenished by the capture of Surat.

He was one of the many tribal soldiers in Chhatrapati Shivaji Maharaj's army. His job was not to get into a direct fight with the enemy. Instead, he would get inside the enemy's house to get their greatest secrets out. He was Bahirji Naik—Chhatrapati Shivaji's best spy. Famed as a 'behrupiya', an impersonator, Bahirji could don any disguise with ease and was entrusted to infiltrate the strongest of enemy camps.

Bahirji believed that in any war, it is as important to have classified information about the enemy as the swords to fight him. But this is not an easy feat. If you are successful, you win; if you don't, you die. But then you are not a great spy if you cannot cheat death.

ADRISHYA

Once a French traveller named Abbé Barthélemy Carré came visiting India. He met an officer of Shivaji and asked, 'What is the secret behind Shivaji Maharaj winning so many wars?' The officer replied, 'He spends a lot of money on his spies. They provide him with all the confidential information about the enemies and Shivaji Maharaj makes his strategies accordingly. And that is how he wins every time.'

There was a time when Shivaji had directly challenged the Mohammed Adil Shah administration, following which an agitated Adil Shah had sworn not to let Shivaji advance against him. Shah then sent a message to Shivaji to this effect, after which the latter immediately called in his best man, Bahirji.

The Maratha period begins from 1630s with the birth of Shivaji. Right from his childhood, Shivaji's ambition was to build an independent state or swaraj. He had witnessed injustice taking place in his own realm/estate (jagir) and nearby areas under the Adil Shah regime. This further strengthened his desire to free commoners and the poor from this abomination.

In 1637, the Nizam Shahi (the rule of the Nizams) got divided and the kingdom disintegrated. The kingdom lay in the north-western Deccan, between the states of Gujarat and Bijapur. While half of it was captured by

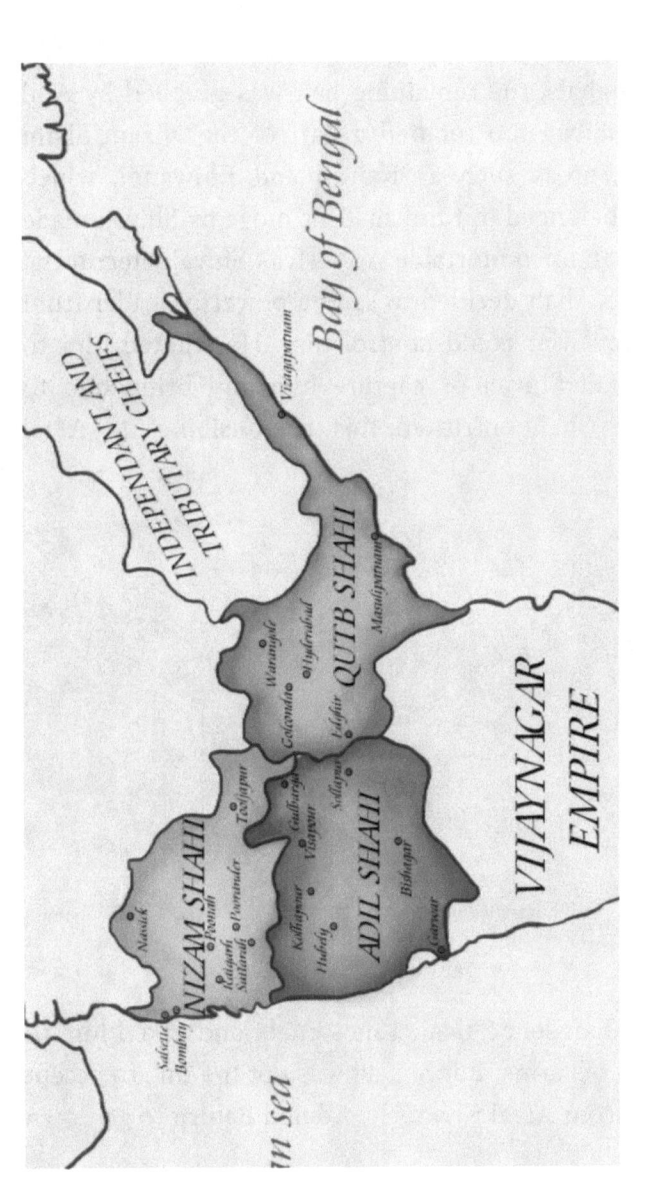

Map of the Nizam kingdom

the Mughals, the remaining half was grabbed by Adil Shah. Shivaji too secured a part of the Nizam Shahi regime, areas such as Kalyan and Bhiwandi, which earlier belonged to Konkan. This move by Shivaji made Adil Shah uncomfortable. To restrict Shivaji's territorial advance, Shah decided to send a powerful leader from his army who could control him. He wanted him to either kill Shivaji or capture him and bring him to Bijapur. Shah entrusted this responsibility to Afzal Khan.

A painting of Afzal Khan

Afzal Khan sent Shivaji a messenger and asked him to give up his arms. But Shivaji was not the one to accept defeat from Afzal Khan. He ordered Bahirji to go down in the jungles of Pratapgad and to keep him informed about the movement of Afzal Khan's army. Bahirji took it as his first big opportunity to prove his competence to Shivaji. Time was running out, but it was not short enough that nothing could be done, he said to himself as he left for the mission.

Bahirji was a common man who belonged to the Ramoshi Bairaj community. Ramoshis were tribal people of Maharashtra who used to live in the jungles around Shivaji's fort. As they spent their lives in the jungle, they were usually very brave. Since they endured so much of hardships and difficulties, they were more warrior-like in their behaviour. It was in these jungles where Bahirji first met Shivaji.

Shivaji was on a tour to understand the activities in his region, but was under disguise. Unaware, Bahirji and his fellow tribesmen warned the strangers by shooting an arrow at them. Shivaji stopped his men from retaliating. He was so impressed by Bahirji's fearlessness and bravery that he invited him to join his army. Bahirji could not guess what Shivaji saw in him to be worthy of such honour. But he felt extremely proud to be trusted by none other than Shivaji himself.

Thus, Bahirji Naik—who was also skilled at donning disguises—started working in Shivaji's army as an impersonator, a spy. His job was to collect the minutest of details about the enemy and send them to Shivaji. Based on Bahirji's inputs, Shivaji would make his strategy.

Bahirji was given the task of getting information from Afzal Khan's camp and was entrusted with the task of finding out their future plans. He reached the camp under disguise. He had thought of meticulous answers to all likely questions that could be asked to him, and had revised them in his mind. There was no scope of any error in this mission.

'I am from the nearby village of Bagalkot, going to the next village. I just wanted to rest for a while. When I saw the bonfire in your camp, I thought I will rest here,' he told Afzal Khan's soldiers as he entered their camp. It was a flawless story, and the soldier at the entrance of the camp believed him without any suspicion. He went inside and asked the soldiers sitting around the bonfire, 'Can I warm my hands here, please?' They obliged him. From the soldiers' gossip, he got to know that Afzal Khan was plotting to kill Shivaji. Little did they know that Bahirji listening to them talk was as good as Shivaji listening himself.

Afzal Khan had fought and won many wars for Adil Shah and the Shah himself wanted such a man to

BAHIRJI NAIK

challenge Shivaji who would instil fear within Shivaji and his army. Khan was full of deceit. He had earlier captured Shivaji's father Shahaji by deceit. He had even killed Shivaji's elder brother, Sambhaji, by deception. He was a shrewd man. His coin had a Persian inscription which read as: *Gar arz kunad sifar ey alaf fazal fazla fazal afzal azhar malke bajaye tazbi awaaz aayat ke afzal afzal.*[1] It can be called wordplay but this couplet is engraved on Afzal Khan's coins, says Ninad Bedekar, a historian who specializes in Maratha history.

Bahirji informed Shivaji that Afzal Khan was creating a ruckus in the plains. When Afzal Khan's army left their base camp, he and his men caused severe damages to numerous temples in Pandharpur and Tarjapur and created a commotion in the area. Khan had intended that on hearing about such destruction and trouble to his people, Shivaji may come down from the Pratapgad Fort and that's when he would engage him in a battle. However, Shivaji did not fall prey to his designs. His spy, Bahirji Naik, who had already infiltrated Afzal Khan's army, had gathered classified information about Khan's plans for Shivaji. From such intelligence, Shivaji understood that if they

---

[1] If the heaven was asked who was the best man on earth, we would hear only one voice from everywhere: It's Afzal, it's Afzal!

could get Khan's big army in the jungles, their battle would become easier. Together Bahirji and Shivaji decided that they would first induce Khan into getting his army in the jungles below the Pratapgad Fort, and then Shivaji would plan his next strategy. They accepted that they were in no position to take on Afzal Khan on the plains. Bahirji then suggested that they should send a message to Afzal Khan, inviting him for a talk till mid-way, and then challenging him there. Duly, a message was sent out and Afzal Khan agreed to the proposition as he was sure of his victory.

However, the message had a few conditions laid out in it for Afzal Khan. One of the terms was that Khan would have to come to the base of the Pratapgad Fort. From there, he would come in a palanquin with ten of his men to a marquee set up at a distance. His men were to stand at a distance of an arrow. Out of ten, only four men would be allowed inside the marquee—Afzal Khan and his lawyer and Shivaji and his lawyer. All these men were allowed to carry their arms. Afzal Khan was happy with the terms because he thought that he would be there in the marquee, armed, with his lawyer and ten men guarding him from outside. So it would not be difficult for him to capture or kill Shivaji.

The day of the meeting was approaching fast. Shivaji's

men were equally motivated by his dream of achieving independence for his people. The way Shivaji used to take every member of his army along with him, his men were fully committed to strive for it, and even sacrifice their lives for it. But that day's challenge was to be played only between Shivaji and Afzal Khan, and Afzal Khan could not be trusted at all. Finally the day of the meeting arrived. It was 10 November 1659. According to the Hindu calendar, it was Margshirsh Shudh Panchami and a Thursday. Shivaji knew that it was the hour of final judgement, and, as always, his self-confidence was his greatest strength at this critical juncture.

When Afzal Khan and Shivaji met under the marquee, Khan, who was taller than Shivaji, wanted to embrace him with open arms. Being a commander in Adil Shah's army, perhaps he wanted to pay his regards to Shivaji who was the son of Shahaji, a leader under Adil Shah. They were already acquainted with each other on this ground. Shivaji walked forward towards Afzal Khan's open arms to hold him into a warm embrace. As soon as they embraced, the smiling Afzal Khan changed into the enemy that he was and tried to strangulate Shivaji who tried to free himself of his grip but couldn't. But Shivaji had not come unprepared. He wore a claw-like sharp weapon on his left hand which he stuck inside

Afzal's back. As Afzal continued strangulating him, Shivaji then attacked him with his knife after which he died on the spot.

It was two in the afternoon when Shivaji killed Afzal Khan.

Soon after Shivaji and his men vanished in the surrounding jungles before Afzal Khan's men could even understand what had happened. Bahirji had already showed them the safest and fastest route to get out of the jungles. After all, he had spent his childhood in these very jungles and knew his way like the back of his hand.

No one had imagined that Shivaji would kill Afzal Khan. This was such a shocking act that it created terror among his enemies. Within the next eighteen days, Shivaji conquered all the areas between Javadi (Pratapgad) and Panargarh. Local chieftains gave away their forts and surrendered; they were petrified that if this man could kill Afzal Khan, he could kill them too. Within the next ten days, which was by 28 November, the whole region came under Shivaji's reign. After that he even conquered the fort of Vishalgad, which was deep inside the forest. That was the day Shivaji's men felt the ecstasy of victory but the credit of these victories didn't go only to Shivaji but also to invisible warriors like Bahirji. It was Bahirji's timely information that had saved Shivaji. But Afzal Khan was not as lucky. Adil Shah's soldiers surrendered without a fight.

Following the news of Shivaji's victory, Aurangzeb sent a huge section of his army towards the Deccan. The general of this army was Shaista Khan who was an able commander and had won many wars. He was very close to the Mughal emperor. With his huge army, Shaista Khan travelled to Pune via Deccan. Once in Pune, Shaista Khan captured Shivaji's childhood home—Lal Mahal—and declared it as his property. Thereafter, the Mughal army started living there.

For three long years, Shaista Khan just stayed put there. In those three years, he captured only the fort of Chakan, named Sangram Durg, and did nothing else. So, Shivaji decided that he would go to him. After all, Shaista Khan had given him a direct challenge by capturing Lal Mahal. Shivaji was angry and restless. He had to give him a suitable reply. Bahirji was looking forward to this direct face-off with the Mughals.

Having spent his childhood there, Shivaji was acquainted with every nook and corner of Lal Mahal. Shivaji's men, including Bahirji, were prepared to go to any length to win it back for him. Once again, the responsibility of planning this mission came on Bahirji's shoulders.

Shivaji had many fond memories of Lal Mahal. Though he had vowed to take it back from Shaista Khan at any cost, it was not an easy feat, as not just Lal Mahal, but the entire Pune region had been surrounded by Shaista Khan and his men. All the entry and exit routes to and from Pune were under strict nakabandi enforced by Shaista Khan. Thus, no Maratha soldier could enter the city. Bahirji Naik at this point suggested to Shivaji that instead of entering as soldiers, if they could enter the city of Pune in any other disguise, they would stand an easy chance to reach Lal Mahal.

Shivaji asked Bahirji what he had in mind. Bahirji said that for a big attack, it was important to get as many soldiers inside the city as possible. Being a spy, he was an expert in disguise. And that's perhaps the reason how he came up with the idea of taking the whole army in disguise to Pune. He thought that they could enter the city on the pretext of a wedding ceremony. He said that this time Shivaji's army would not move forward on a sly, but dancing and singing.

There was an army of seventy thousand in Pune, and in the middle of it was Shaista Khan. This was the time of the holy month of Ramzan. So the Mughal soldiers would fast during the day, have their one meal in the evening and go to sleep. Shivaji chose a day during this month and planned to strike at night when the soldiers were asleep.

Shivaji and Bahirji's men, who disguised themselves as baraatis (part of a wedding procession), managed to enter the city as they were not stopped by anyone. In the enveloping darkness of the night, they managed to sneak into Lal Mahal quite easily. Bahirji knew that they wouldn't have won against Khan's one thousand soldiers guarding the Mahal in a direct fight. But Shaista Khan's soldiers couldn't defend themselves against this sudden attack, and Shivaji's men had a gala 'wedding celebration'.

Prior to this attack, Shivaji's spies had provided him with all the crucial details about Shaista Khan: like where he stays, how many people were around him and what were their individual roles. And without any doubt, Bahirji Naik had led this network of spies.

Shaista Khan paid a heavy price in this attack—his son, his four fingers, his self-respect and, of course, the Lal Mahal of Pune.

It was evident that Shivaji's war strategy and tactics were quite different from Afzal Khan and Shaista Khan. Nobody could have thought of this strategy which he used against Shaista Khan. A strategy's success depends on planning, and planning in turn depends on information. There is no room for doubt that Shivaji had a reliable network of spies. It was this network that helped him drag Shaista Khan out of Pune.

Shivaji's strategy is called Ganimi Kawa (guerrilla warfare), also known as Shiva Sutra. It was a strategy which was very different from others. All of Shivaji's enemies—be it Bijapur's Adil Shahi or the Mughals—were experts in ground battle. Shivaji had realized that his army was not ready for a direct battle with them. Therefore, he adopted a strategy of attacking his enemies when they were least expecting it. To be able to follow this strategy, it was important for him to have as much classified information about his enemy as possible and the task of gathering such critical intelligence was done by spies like Bahirji.

Bahirji understood that a war was an expensive affair and required money and other resources regularly. Even Shivaji's army was no longer a small one like it used to be earlier. It was not an easy task to look after an army of about one lakh soldiers. Although Shivaji had thrown Shaista Khan out of Pune, his coffers had almost run dry coping with the destruction done by Shaista Khan over the last three years.

Now, Shivaji had no money left and his kingdom

was in shambles. It had become imperative to replenish his treasury. There is a sentence in a Marathi chronicle which says, *Surat mareli ani agrit dravya saple.* This means that if one can plunder the city of Surat, he would get unimaginable wealth there. The prevalent belief was that if they could win just one village in Surat, they would be able to overcome the sum of losses incurred in fighting Afzal Khan and the three years of destruction done by Shaista Khan.

Shivaji was trying to find a solution for this financial crisis. Bahirji was clearer; he knew they should take the road to Surat. Surat was under the reign of Aurangzeb's sister and was brimming with wealth. When Bahirji discussed his plan with Shivaji, the latter immediately made up his mind about attacking Surat. But to achieve that, he needed to get a sense about the security measures in place at Surat. Once again, Shivaji assigned the risky task to Bahirji Naik.

In his earlier days, during his travels around the Mughal areas, Bahirji had gone to Surat as well. He had noticed the abundance of wealth in the city and knew that such wealth could consolidate more power and strength for the Marathas. It was obvious that this time he could not enter the city of Surat as a Maratha warrior or even as a representative of the Maratha army. So he

Surat, bustling with trade

visited the city donning the disguise of a gondhadi.[2]

Surat was a big city and thus its security measures were equally big. Under Inayat Khan's administration, tax was collected from the businessmen of the city. People going on Haj also used to give him money as taxes. Surat, hence, was considered a shrimant shahar (a prosperous city). Subedar Inayat Khan, being the commander of Surat, was extremely aware of his position and was an arrogant man. As a result, power had gone to his head. With a taste for music and dance, he was used to being surrounded by sycophants all day long. He was a lazy man with a rangeen mizaz (fancy taste) and Bahirji knew exactly how this weakness could be exploited. Bahirji's whole disguise drama was done especially for him. He, however, was aware that his trick may fall flat and tables could turn in front of the Mughal soldiers' might. Bahirji knew that his plan of entering Surat as a spy was going to be extremely risky for him and his accomplices (two real Gondhal artistes); it was a matter of life and death. His entire strategy hinged on just one belief that soldiers usually had a soft corner for artists and singers. Their most critical task was to convince them that they actually were folk singers.

---

[2] Gondhadis were a section of Marathas who used to earn their living by telling folk stories to people.

Inayat Khan himself was quite knowledgeable about music. He asked Bahirji to sing. Bahirji, who had come fully prepared, had brought two real Gondhadi artistes with him. They performed with ease and convinced Inayat Khan that they were musicians indeed. Inayat Khan was happy and even rewarded them.

That was the time for the next step. As a Gondhadi artiste, Bahirji got friendly with the Mughal soldiers and slowly extracted information about the city, Surat, the routes to and fro to it and the city plan.

Once the surveillance of Surat city was done, Bahirji and his associates escaped from the city. Shivaji was eagerly waiting for the crucial details they had gathered.

Bahirji had worked exceptionally well this time. He prepared and provided a blueprint of his plan to Shivaji. They had every possible information on Surat with them—how Surat was; how its ports were; who the richest people were in Surat; and who had how much money with them and where exactly they had kept it, whether plastered inside the wall or under the ground or in the almirahs. Bahirji Naik might have even known how much these men carried in their pockets!

After Inayat Khan realized what had happened, he was furious. He was particularly angry at the fact that Shivaji's men had spied upon him after entering his house. Shivaji had in a way silently arrived at his doorstep. He called his best soldier and gave him the special task to go to Shivaji as his messenger. Once he arrived at Shivaji's court, Shivaji thought that he must be a regular messenger and had come with an offer of some money from Inayat Khan or a tribute.

Though the messenger Kasim Khan had come as an emissary of peace, Bahirji was aware that he was an exceptional warrior; so he was sceptical of his intentions. While Kasim came to meet Shivaji, Bahirji who was also present there, kept a close watch on him. When Kasim tried to attack Shivaji, Bahirji attacked Kasim and killed him. By trying to attack Shivaji, Inayat Khan had now made a terrible mistake.

Within no time Shivaji and his army attacked Surat and achieved what they had set out for. The victory over Surat provided them with an abundance of wealth and offered them a new lease for their future plans. The war with Surat was not their last war; several wars were fought and won after that. And Bahirji kept playing a crucial role in Shivaji's journey as a ruler. Bahirji considered it his privilege to be able to walk shoulder-to-shoulder with him. Shivaji, in turn, bestowed Bahirji with the title of 'Sartaj'. This was a matter of not only great pride for Bahirji but also for all his fellow tribesmen from Ramoshi community.

Spies such as Bahirji and Shivaji Maharaj's other commanders played a huge role in the Chhatrapati's legendary success. In history, success stories of rulers, kings, rajas and chhatrapatis are known to all. However, history doesn't say much about those people who have followed their masters' strategies, worked alongside them, done the necessary groundwork and even made enormous sacrifices. Unfortunately, these are the lesser-known voices of history.

Painting of Shivaji attacking Surat

EXPERTS

Ninad Bedekar is a historian who specializes in Maratha history. An orator and a writer, Bedekar is well versed with documents from Shivaji's period and is actively involved in protecting historical monuments of India.

Dr Sonali Pednekar is the Head of Department (History), V.G. Vaze College of Arts, Science and Commerce, Mumbai. Her area of specialization is Maratha history.

5

Sharan Kaur

The Warrior Spy
(19th century)

Sharni was a sixteen-year-old Hindu girl from North West Frontier Province. Life changed forever when she was kidnapped on her wedding day, while on the way to her new home, by a group of fierce dacoits. Sharni was freed by the army of Hari Singh Nalwa, the great commander of the Sikh empire. Grateful to Nalwa for having freed her from perennial doom, Sharni adopted Sikhism and was rechristened Sharangat Kaur, a Khalsa warrior and a shrewd spy. At a time when Nalwa was battling the ferocious Pathan tribes of the northeast and their cruel leader, Dost Mohammad, Sharan braved to go where no Sikh man would go. Entering Pathan camps, she gathered information about Dost Mohammad's strategy and brought them over to Nalwa. Her devotion to the Sikh empire continued even after Nalwa's death, where she braved the Pathan army surrounding the Sikh fort of Jamrud in Khyber Pass and travelled all the way to Lahore on foot by herself, killing all those who came in her way. The transformation of this delicate girl into a proud member of the Sikh army is known only through old Sikh folk tales that are sung around the country under various names of Sharan Kaur, Sharangat Kaur and Bibi Sharan Kaur.

The story of Sharan Kaur starts in 1834, when the Sikh Empire in India was at its peak. Maharaja Ranjit Singh had built an empire which was dreaded by the Afghans, the East India Company and even the Russians on the other side. His kingdom stretched from Sutlej to Khyber Pass, from Kashmir in the north to Sindh in the south and till Tibet in the east. Hari Singh Nalwa, a very able general of the Sikh kingdom, was an administrator of the Peshawar and Rawalpindi region. He was the commander-in-chief of Maharaja Ranjit Singh along the Afghan frontier.

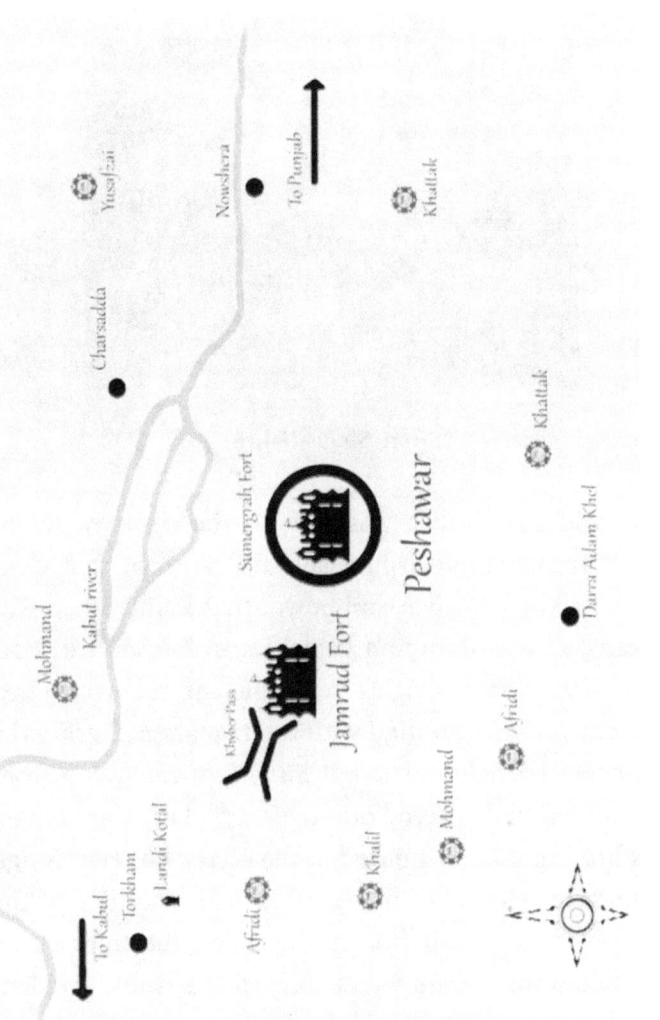

Map of Peshawar

ADRISHYA

Hari Singh Nalwa

It is said that Nalwa was sent to the court of Ranjit Singh regarding a dispute about a land. In that case, he showed such talent and power that Ranjit Singh was impressed with him and kept him in his service. Hari Singh was probably eighteen or nineteen years old when one day he went hunting with the maharaja. During the hunt, Hari Singh and Ranjit Singh got separated from the others and a ferocious tiger attacked Hari Singh. His horse got badly injured in the attack but Hari Singh did not lose hope; with a small kripan (a knife that the Sikhs keep on their bodies) he killed the tiger all by himself. Ranjit Singh was watching the whole incident unfold and when he killed the tiger, it is said that Ranjit Singh said, '*Wah mere Raja Nal*', which means 'Well done, my King Nal'. It was after this incident that others in Ranjit Singh's court started calling Hari Singh with the name of Nalwa.

Sharan Kaur was born as Sharni in a Brahmin household. Her village was near Jamrud Fort in Khyber Pass. On the day of her wedding, when she was on her way to her in-law's place through a jungle in a doli (palanquin), her baraat (marriage procession) got attacked by robbers. They tried pulling Sharni out of her palanquin. Scared and terrified, Sharni tried to escape as fast as possible from the attackers. But she knew her legs would not carry her too far. Suddenly something happened that made the bandits stop in their tracks. Fear was writ large on their faces. When Sharni looked back, she saw Sikh soldiers blocking the dacoits. They rounded up the attackers and killed them all, thus saving Sharni's honour and life. Relieved and grateful, Sharni was deeply impressed by the valour and heroism of the Khalsa Sikhs. She realized that she wanted to be like them, taking the reins of her life in her own hands, and not depend on anyone else for her safety.

The Sikh soldiers, after saving Sharni, brought her to the court of Hari Singh Nalwa.

ADRISHYA

It is said that because the Afghans had faced defeat in the hands of the Sikhs in an open battle, they found a way to get some wealth by attacking marriage processions and taking away the bride and looting all the money, jewellery and whatever else they could lay their hands on.

Sharni realized that as she was abducted she could neither go and live with her husband and in-laws nor go back to her parents as her honour would be questioned after the abduction. When Sardar Hari Singh Nalwa asked her what her name was, she did not know what to reply. For her, Sharni had died by then; her old life was a distant memory changed by the events of the last few days. She was dead for the world since she had been abducted by the dacoits. The Sardar then gave her a new name, saying that since she had come to his sharan (refuge), she would be called 'Sharan Kaur' from that day. After the traumatic incident in the jungle, Sharan understood that a life which is lived with bravery is a life well lived. Also, it was not enough to be just good and truthful; one should have the strength to end injustice and lies in this world. Now with a new lease of life, she too wanted to achieve that strength and power, but the question was, how. How could she make Hari Singh believe that a woman could also be a part of his army?

It is believed that because she was named 'Kaur', she converted to Sikhism. To become a Sikh, she had to taste amrit, which she must have done, and when one tastes amrit, it is said that a different kind of energy flows through him/her, a special kind of power and strength which helps the Sikhs to fight for justice, to save people and to fight against injustice. The person becomes a soldier for a cause and when one is a combination of a soldier and a Sikh, one gets the power to shake the world. Guru Gobind Singh, the last of the Sikh gurus, showed the Sikhs this path through which they felt empowered. He made them believe that one Khalsa (Sikh) is equal to one and a quarter lakh people. On the basis of this belief, the Sikhs achieved many conquests which, if one thinks rationally, were impossible to win.

After giving refuge to Sharan, Hari Singh Nalwa handed over some responsibilities to her; however, these were all kitchen duties. She knew she did not just belong in the kitchen and with her intelligence, she could even hold the reins of an army. One day, Hari Singh Nalwa was walking around that area when he saw that a vessel getting dropped from someone's hand was quickly caught in mid-air by Sharan. Seeing her quick reflex, the Sardar felt that she had something in her which made her special. He remembered that Sharan had told him earlier as to how she was in awe of the Sikh soldiers and wanted to become like them. The Sardar made up his mind then that she should become a soldier, thus granting her biggest wish. On his orders, Sharan started her training to be a soldier in his army.

The first day she held a sword, she understood the aim of her life. She was a soldier at heart and was born for that purpose. Looking at the Sikh soldiers in the army, she used to dream of becoming like them. She never missed out on training. Probably she felt that this was the time when she could devote her life to this community, fight the enemies and give back as much as possible to the Sikh society.

During the training, Sharan Kaur was taught sword fighting and other techniques of warfare. When she, a lone girl, was training with four male soldiers, she used to fight as if the duel was real. Hari Singh Nalwa noticed her keen enthusiasm and thought that her energy and zeal should be channelized in a proper manner.

As her training came to an end, the Sardar told her about the Afghan camps around the region. She learnt that Hari Singh Nalwa had defeated the Khyberi Pathans for the first time in Jamrud and it was such a terrible defeat that the Afghans were terrified of even the name of the Sardar. However, the Afghans were raring to avenge themselves and wanted to defeat the Sikh kingdom. The principal among these were chiefs Dost Mohammad and Akbar Ali. Both were known to be ferocious and cruel.

Dost Mohammad

With his power and capability, Hari Singh Nalwa had kept the Afghans away from the Sikh kingdom for quite a long time. He was famed as the man who could kill a tiger with his bare hands; so his valour was widely known. Just the mention of his name was enough to suppress his enemies; such was the terror he created in his foes.

Sharan noticed that Sardar Nalwa was quiet since the last few days. It appeared that he was thinking of something. When she asked him several times on what was bothering him, he replied that he wanted to know what was going on in the Afghan camps. She told him that she would go there and, to her surprise, he agreed. She had got her first mission. It was time when she could go amidst the Pathans and prove that she could even die for her clan.

It is one thing to have inborn talent and natural guts, but to channelize them in the constructive manner you need the right people guiding you to your path. Sharan was very fortunate in this as she got to work alongside an able warrior like Hari Singh Nalwa. He had spotted her talent and the zeal which drove her to achieve something great.

Twenty miles away from Jamrud, there were many small Afghani camps. Akbar Ali had a big camp there as well. Sharan Kaur was brought up in the nearby region and could speak Pashto well. The Sardar decided that Sharan was the right person who could gather information from this camp. Disguised as an Afghan woman, she approached the Afghan camp. The Afghani soldiers stopped her but on seeing a pitiable woman, they let her in to meet Akbar Ali.

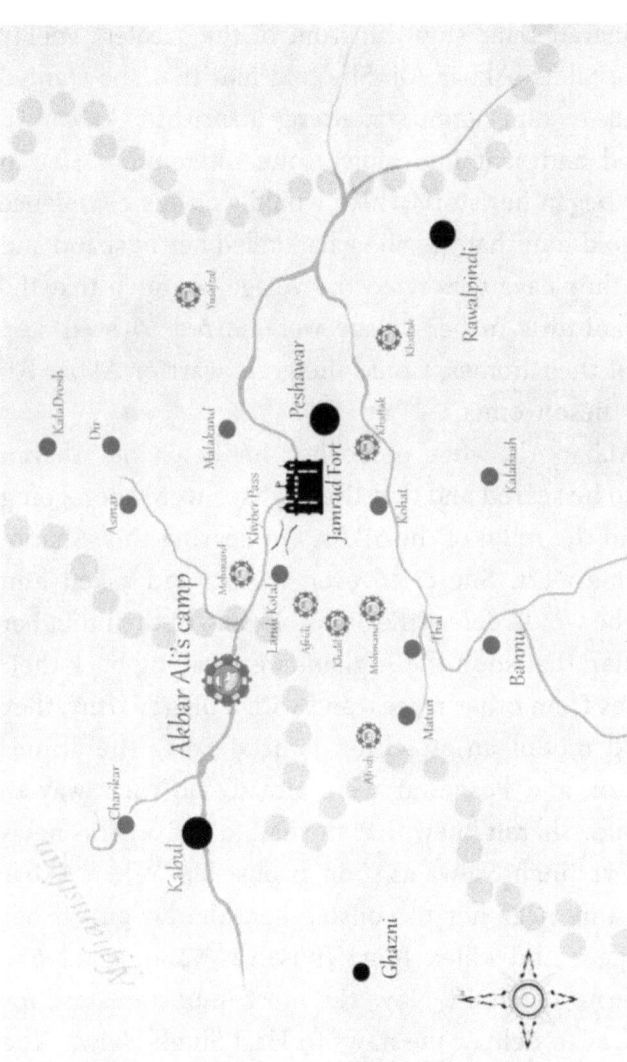

Map depicting the location of Jamrud Fort and Akbar Ali's camp

ADRISHYA

Sharan Kaur stood in front of the greatest enemy of the Sikhs, Akbar Ali. She told him that she wanted to talk to him about something in private. Akbar Ali agreed and sent his soldiers out. Thereupon, Sharan Kaur began her story which would gain his confidence and told him that the Sikhs had killed her husband and how they have terrorized the village so much that the Afghani girls in her village were scared to even step out of their homes. Could the great warrior Akbar Ali help these women?

Akbar Ali, when beseeched for help, told Sharan not to be scared and that the Afghans were soon going to end the reign of the Sikhs. On hearing this, Sharan became alert. She cried even harder and asked him how he would defeat the Sikhs. Akbar Ali then told her his plan that soon the Afghans were calling back their armies from other places, and with a bigger army, they would mount an attack on Jamrud Fort. The armies of Atok and Peshawar were already on their way to Jamrud. Sharan knew that she had to deliver this news to Hari Singh Nalwa as soon as possible. When Akbar Ali came near her to console her, Sharan pulled out a dagger and killed him. Thus was vanquished one powerful chieftain. Now, the most important task for her was to deliver the news to Hari Singh Nalwa. The only fear was of her getting noticed.

Sharan changed her disguise from a young Afghan woman to an old Afghan woman; she came out and disappeared into the crowd. On discovering that Akbar Ali was dead, the soldiers came out and started looking for that girl everywhere but could not find her. When they found an old woman, Sharan in disguise, and asked her if she had seen a young girl go by, she replied in the negative.

Thus escaping, Sharan went back and delivered the complete information to Hari Singh Nalwa.

Meanwhile, the sudden death of Akbar Ali created a chaos in the Afghan army. Seizing this perfect moment, the soldiers of Hari Singh Nalwa attacked them. The Afghans were not ready for an attack and they fled. Victorious, in front of the whole court, Sardar Hari Singh honoured Sharan Kaur. She cried their war cry:

Jo bole so nihaal!
Sat Sri Akal!

From that day onwards she became a trusted soldier and spy of Hari Singh Nalwa. With Akbar Ali's death the danger got averted for sometime but they could not drop their guard yet. Many a times she was sent to deliver secret messages, take rounds outside the fort or bring information from other territories. She carried out every task with a great amount of zeal. The kingdom was safe but gradually Hari Singh Nalwa's health was deteriorating and with that Sharan's responsibilities were increasing. Amidst all that, a piece of good news arrived—the wedding of Maharaja Ranjit Singh's grandson, Nau Nihal Singh. Along with the British, Maharaja Ranjit Singh also invited the Afghan leader, Dost Mohammad to the wedding.

Portrait of Maharaja Ranjit Singh

Maharaja Ranjit Singh wanted to have a grand wedding for his grandson. He wanted the world to see his power and bravery and wanted to create a fear in the hearts of others. It is said that Nau Nihal Singh's wedding celebrations continued for two months in the cities of Amritsar and Lahore.

All senior leaders were invited for the wedding, including the British Commander-in-Chief of India General Henry Fane. The maharaja wanted to impress the Englishmen gathered with the Sikh army, and so he called all his soldiers who were deployed elsewhere to Amritsar and Lahore. Dost Mohammad came to the wedding too but he sent all five of his sons to re-group his army from all small camps and attack the Sikhs. Hari Singh Nalwa was in the Sumergarh Fort and some historians suggest that he was sick at that time.

Having attended the wedding, Dost Mohammad started towards Jamrud Fort with his army. He was aware that Sardar Hari Singh Nalwa was not there. He had gone to Bala Hissar, near Peshwar, for his treatment. It was not possible for Sharan Kaur to fight the war alone and had something happened to Jamrud while she was in charge, she would have fallen in her own eyes. There were several Pathan camps around Jamrud Fort which were happy under the reign of the Sikhs. But to occupy the fort, Dost Mohammad wanted them all to join him. His terror was such that the tribals were scared to refute his orders. Now there was only one way to fight the Afghans: if somehow Sardar Hari

The wedding procession of Nau Nihal Singh

Singh Nalwa could get back to Jamrud. His name alone was enough to scare Dost Mohammad and his army. But how was he to be informed when he was miles away? The environment around the fort was getting dangerous. The Afghan army was coming closer with every minute. Stepping out of the fort was like inviting death for dinner. But the right thing had to be done and so deciding that, Sharan Kaur stepped out.

The Afghans were waiting in every direction for an attack. Sharan Kaur could not shake off the feeling that someone was following her. And she was right. But the one whose saviour is God cannot be killed by anyone. God, once again, was on her side.

The journey which Sharan Kaur travelled between Bala Hissar and Jamrud was a very difficult one and the Afghans were all over the route. Evading all these soldiers, a lone girl riding a horse—crossing the jungles, threading through the silence—reached Bala Hissar to meet Hari Singh Nalwa.

Seeing the Sardar so sick, Sharan did not want to ask him to go with her. But she could not hide the truth of the situation from him and hence informed him about what had been taking place in Jamrud all this time. On hearing the grave danger, the Sardar assured her that he would definitely go with her to save Jamrud and asked her to go and prepare for the return journey.

Hari Singh Nalwa did not wait for the army to return from Lahore. He got up, even though he was ill, collected his people, and in the middle of the night itself, moved towards Jamrud with his army. On the morning of 30 April 1837, he reached the battlefield. As soon as the Afghans saw him, they were petrified. They had never thought that Hari Singh Nalwa would come from Peshawar. They ran away from the field and hid in the surrounding caves of the area. Suddenly another unit of Afghans came to the battleground from Khyber

Pass. They were clueless about what was happening in the battlefield and when they saw the Sikhs, they attacked them, in which Hari Singh Nalwa got badly injured.

The battle scene of the troops of
Hari Singh Nalwa and the Afghans

Sharan Kaur quickly took Hari Singh Nalwa into the Jamrud Fort. But Hari Singh Nalwa, the man who had given Sharan a new lease of life, was now no more. He was not just her Sardar, but was also her guru. Seeing him dead was like the end of the world for Sharan Kaur. She felt that she had lost the shelter and the empowering hand from above her head. But she did not lose hope. It was her responsibility as well to save the fort. But with the death of Hari Singh Nalwa, his dead body in front of her, Sharan knew that this update should not reach outside because if the news spread, it would be a huge disappointment for the Sikhs. They would be too demoralized to fight the Afghans and not only Jamrud, other portions of the Sikh kingdom might be lost too.

The enemy was not far away. The one thing which was stopping them was the belief that Sardar Hari Singh Nalwa was sitting inside the fort, like a tiger, protecting it. Had the Afghans got to know about his death, it wouldn't have taken them long to seize Jamrud. Sharan however had to deliver this piece of information at the earliest to Maharaja Ranjit Singh in Lahore. But before that she wanted the Afghan fear of the Sardar to still continue to buy more time for herself.

Afghan soldiers keeping a watch

According to folk tales, Hari Singh's body was cleansed from inside and embalmed and preserved. Sharan then suggested that he be made to sit on a horse (as he could not sit on a horse so he was tied to it) and then be taken for a round in the fort once a day. This way the Afghans could see from far away that Hari Singh Nalwa was alive. Whatever the trick was, it kept the Afghans to believe that probably Hari Singh Nalwa was alive. The Afghan army was now in doubt and kept standing outside the small fort of Jamrud, without attacking, not just for a day or two, but for ten days. Only a handful of people knew about his demise. However, Sharan knew that the lie could not sustain for too long. She had to somehow inform Maharaja Ranjit Singh about these developments. Again the question was who would take the news to him? Folk tales suggest that Sharan again volunteered for this dangerous mission. She said she would go and nobody would doubt her. She also reasoned that because she was small, she wouldn't be easily sighted, and because she had no beard, she could also pass off as a young boy. So, she disguised herself and delivered the news to Ranjit Singh.

Hari Singh Nalwa was Maharaja Ranjit Singh's favoured general and he was shocked when he heard of his death. He promised that he himself would take

SHARAN KAUR

his army to Jamrud. When the Afghans got to know that the whole army of Ranjit Singh had reached Peshawar, they got terrified. His attack was so ferocious that Dost Mohammad and his army ran back to Kabul without even putting up a fight.

In the battle that Maharaja Ranjit Singh fought, Sharan Kaur was shoulder to shoulder with him and once again Jamrud was saved by her. She proved her capability and dutifully performed her role of a spy. After the victory of Jamrud, Maharaja Ranjit Singh honoured Sharan in his court and rewarded her with a sword. This further increased Sharan Kaur's responsibilities. He wanted her to train other soldiers and make them spies like her—teach them the duties of a spy, how to have better observation skills, etc.—so that she would be instrumental in creating more Sharan Kaurs for his army.

Sharan wondered at times that had she remained Sharni and not become Sharan Kaur, what would her life be? If the bandits had not robbed her palanquin, how would her life been? Had her story not taken that poor turn then, would it have taken such a great shape later?

The victory of Jamrud was not the end. That was the starting for Sharan Kaur, of her new life, of preparing new soldiers and spies, which she did magnificently.

Maharaja Ranjit Singh died in 1939. But by that

time, many girls like Sharan Kaur had become a part of his army.

EXPERTS

Vanit Nalwa is the seventh-generation descendant of Sardar Hari Singh Nalwa and is the author of *Hari Singh Nalwa: Champion of the Khalsaji 1791–1837*, which attempts to compile her forefather's history through folk songs, journals of British secret agents and popular history.

Dr Ravinder K. Cheema is an assistant professor at the Department of History, Guru Nanak Khalsa College of Arts, Science and Commerce, Mumbai.

6

Aziz-Un-Nisa

The Courtesan Spy
(19th century)

When India fought its First War of Independence in 1857, military towns across the country rose against the gross injustice of the British. Along with the rebels, a large number of civilians too joined the cause, including members of kothas. These were entertainment centres that doubled up as custodians of Indian culture and tehzeeb. With their Indian patrons—nawabs and kings— being termed immoral, the courtesans themselves were treated like common prostitutes, and kothas became brothels for British officers. Enraged by her degraded condition, Aziz-Un-Nisa—a courtesan who had travelled

ADRISHYA

from the cultural capital of Lucknow to the gritty city of Kanpur just to be independent—decided to fight against the British. She started out as a spy, entering parties and passing on information about her British patrons to the rebels, sheltering the rebels and later even actively participated in the planning of the uprising. It is still sung about in the city of Kanpur that among the rebels that fought on the side of Peshwa Nana Saheb was a beautiful courtesan spy who had taken up arms for her own independence and that of her country.

Aziz-Un's complete name was Aziz-Un-Nisa. In today's time when people do not know how to pronounce her name correctly, they call her Ajijan Bai but her name Aziz-Un comes from the Urdu word 'aziz', which means 'close to the heart'.

The first memory that Aziz-Un had of her childhood was the tinkle of ankle-bells. She was brought up in an environment of music and dance. Her mother used to affectionately ask her, 'Don't your feet hurt? You have been dancing all day. At least have your food or is even that not in your destiny?' But her food was different; it was the lyrics of the songs, the sound of the tabla and the tinkling of ankle-bells which were all she cared about.

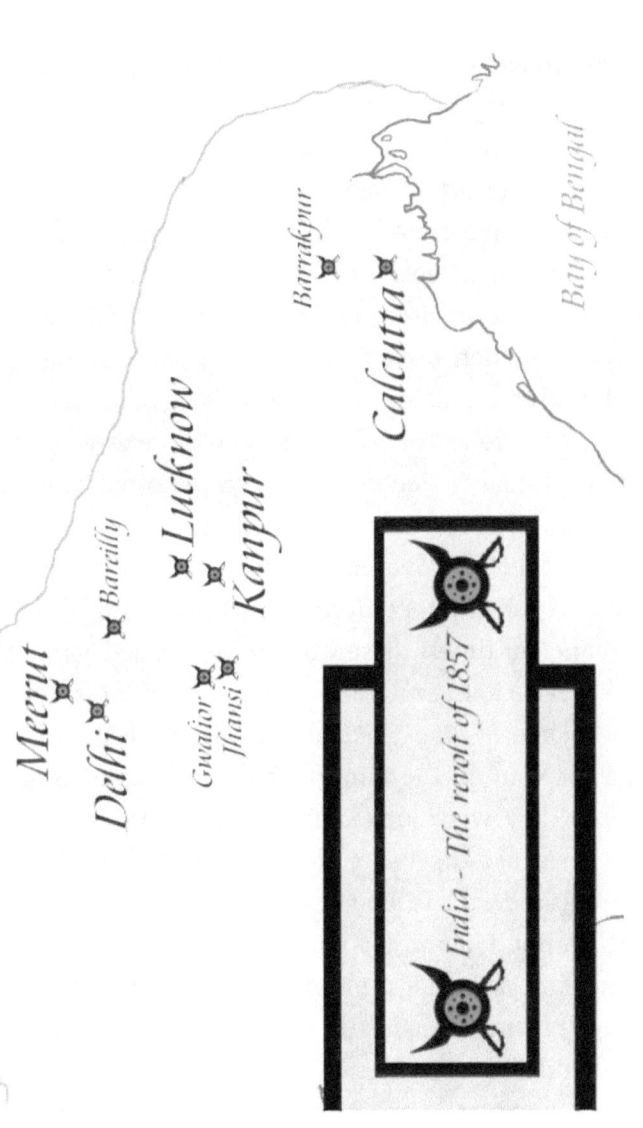

Map depicting the areas which raged in the fire of the revolt of 1857

ADRISHYA

The concept of kothas as we now understand is incorrect, twisted by the passage of time. During those days, they were considered as kalakendras (centres of art) where the art of singing, poetry and dance was learnt from childhood. Women practising this art used to call themselves fan-kara or adakara (artists or performers). They used to learn to write and recite as well. The women used to meet other men inside the kothas and exchange views, words, writings and opinions with them. The art of conversation was believed to be of the best quality. People used to go to kothas to learn how to sit, talk, communicate intelligently and listen to what was being conveyed. In effect, kothas were the centres of social interaction.

In ancient times, these women were called 'ganikas'. Ganikas have found mention in Jain and Buddhist texts, in Sudraka's *Mrichhakatika* and in Arthashashtra. They had a place in all the important documents of Indian culture. They were looked upon with respect by the society because they were considered cultural women. There was indeed a feeling of uneasiness regarding their sexuality. But if one would read about King Bimbisara or the ancient city of Magadha and the story of Nagarvadhu Amrapali from Vaishali, and even a few Buddhist texts, they would know that these women commanded respect in the society, at social, religious or other functions.

AZIZ-UN-NISA

The most important thing is that these women were also politically inclined.

As Aziz-Un grew up in the environment of kothas frequented by the nawabs, she developed a strong disliking for nawabi behaviour—greedy, lusty and violent. The nawabs held positions of great political power in Lucknow. It was getting difficult for Aziz-Un to escape from their clutches. She did not wish to live as someone's servant—neither the nawabs' nor the British's. Her dream was to earn a dignified living, even if that was not lavish.

Lucknow was home to Wajid Ali Shah, who had his own harem of beautiful girls and women, and had Aziz-Un wanted she could have been a part of the nawabi harem. She was after all a tawaif (courtesan) who was an expert in the art of singing and dancing. But she left Lucknow and came to Kanpur, even if that meant starting her life from scratch. She didn't even go to Bithur where Nana Saheb had his flourishing and big household. She came to Kanpur because she wanted to establish her own independent kotha.

In Kanpur, there was a lot of military presence during that time. There were men from the British army of the East India Company. She established herself there as a courtesan afresh. She was no more a dependent on a nawab or any other rich patron. She had a streak of independent thinking; so she was brave enough to establish her own kotha in the middle of a bustling market in Kanpur. Though she knew that most people attending her kotha would not understand her art, it was just an excuse for her to rehearse. This way she was also free to meet and converse with clients of her own choosing, share her views and opinions with the men who were fond of her and have a life where she chose whom she met.

Shamshuddin Savaar is believed to be one of those men who were close to Aziz-Un. He had first met Aziz-Un in Kanpur. He was a rider in the forty-second cavalry. He used to earn a decent living and there were several men who were under him. The armies at that time were not as organized as they are today; there used to be different groups within them. He was in charge of one such group. He was known to be a very courageous and generous man. Shamshuddin was a frequent visitor at Aziz-Un's kotha, and it is believed that they were very fond of each other.

It was now the late 1850s. A storm was brewing inside Shamshuddin's chest these days. Being a soldier in the Company army, he had given his utmost to the British. But in return, they had hurt his and Aziz-Un's religious sentiments, as the British had recently issued new cartridges which were wrapped in paper greased with cow and pig fat. These had to be opened by the soldier with his mouth. This thus affected the religious sensibilities of both Hindu and Muslim members of the army. Shamshuddin was enraged by this new rule and took up the cause to revolt; Aziz-Un too was affected by his sentiment.

After the Mangal Pandey incident, the people of his regiment had rebelled and spread all over the region. They went to different cantonments and informed people about Pandey's story, which in turn fuelled the rage against the British. This disenchantment touched Aziz-Un as well, as she must have heard about the incident from her patrons. The episode of Mangal Pandey had become an important reference for everybody.

British soldiers blowing up rebel sepoys in front of canons

ADRISHYA

※

Kanpur was the hub of British cantonment. Sometimes when visiting Aziz-Un's kotha, the East India Company soldiers would make plans of their next battles; this way she came into a position where she could gather information about their ideas and plans. Various kinds of people used to visit her kotha, and with them they would bring different kinds of news. Aziz-Un used to wait for such news. One way to do it was to listen to them talk when they would be at her place. If they sounded scared, apprehensive or if they were talking of going to some other place or collecting ration in bulk, these were indications of something brewing. She could understand that there was some threat to their security or they were planning something which could have a reaction. She could get such information out and pass it on to Shamshuddin and his comrades.

When she went out to give some information, she would feel she was being followed. But she knew that it was important for her to pass on the secret information to Shamshuddin. On reaching him, before words could transpire, they hugged each other. Shamshuddin was surprised on seeing her, and wondered how she managed to reach him in the darkness of the night. But danger was in the shadows and she had to brave the risk to have a word with him. She told him that a British officer was roaming freely after shooting an Indian soldier and was boasting unabashedly about it at her kotha. Shamshuddin knew about it; he and his men were itching for revenge. That night Shamshuddin told her that the day was not far when the British would mourn for their friend's death and Indians would watch and enjoy the show. He also told her that Nana Saheb was coming to Kanpur with a huge army. That was the night which marked a clear path for Aziz-Un in this mission. It was her heartiest desire to breathe the fresh air of this free nation.

Aziz-Un was a woman of independent views, and she was in love with Shamshuddin. Shamshuddin himself was a mutineer who, after coming under the influence of Nana Saheb, had started working against the British army. Naturally, his political leanings started influencing and shaping Aziz-Un's thoughts as well. It was believed that Shamshuddin Savaar had left some impression on Aziz-Un. But again, because she was an independent-thinking woman, she also took many decisions by her own self. So it must have been her personal choice to be a part of the mutiny which was why she was there. It would not be correct to assume that Aziz-Un became a part of the whole affair only because Shamshuddin asked her to be. Aziz-Un-Nisa was happy that her life was blessed with both love and a motive. She was proud of who they were and their objective.

The courtesans had to pay tax to the government. Every month, on a fixed date, Aziz-Un used to reach the police station without being called. But now, she was particularly conscious about what she heard. Every conversation was information for her. Everything was of importance to the nation. She had got the hint that something was going to happen in the days to come. This news was of use to her and her fellow mutineers.

Shamshuddin was in touch with all the big leaders of the revolt of 1857, such as Tatya Tope and Nana Saheb, and used to attend all meetings held by them. Some of these meetings were also held at Aziz-Un's house. Very soon her kotha become a crucial spot in the planning and execution of the revolt. It had started witnessing, along with singing and dancing, the maps of an uprising. Aziz-Un believed that every revolt started from the house and then reached the crossing of the market; once it was there, it could not be stopped. She loved her motherland as much as the Indian sepoys loved their country.

The art of spying cannot be taken lightly. It is a very dangerous job. When you fight a war, you have

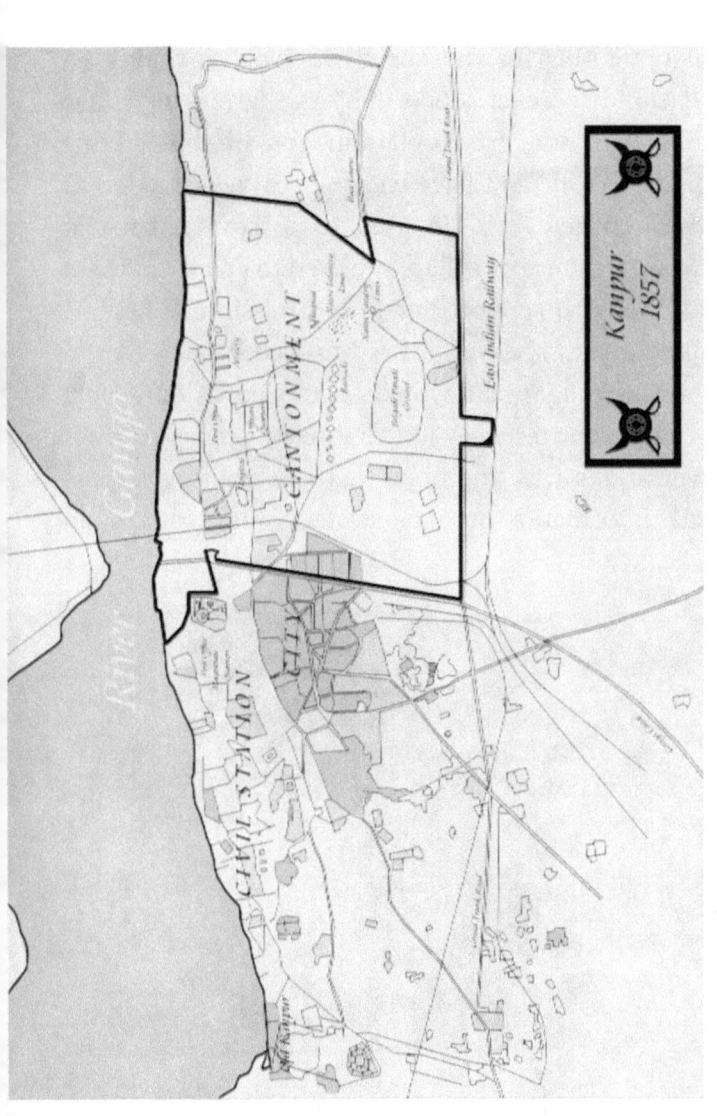

Map of Kanpur, 1857

soldiers fighting for you and beside you. A soldier on the ground is never alone; he has a group of fellow soldiers with him, even a platoon. You are dressed in a soldier's armour and have weapons to defend yourself with. But when Aziz-Un used to go spying, be it at somebody's house or a club, she used to go alone. There was nobody to support her in her mission. Whatever would happen, she would have to face it on her own. If she was caught, she would have been killed. Going into the enemy territory like that to eavesdrop on their conversations with the hope that she would get some special information or some strategy was a very tough and risky job.

Nana Saheb   Tatya Tope

One day she was called by the Officer's Club for a performance which she accepted. Her performance in the previous year had earned her much appreciation. She was beautiful and was proficient in the art of endearment and seduction. However, Shamsuddin was not sure about Aziz-Un being up to the task. Or perhaps he was concerned about her safety, and so didn't want her to come to the Officer's Club that night. The task at hand was dangerous but Aziz-Un knew that only she could do it. But she was so cautious and discreet during her performance that even her left eyelash did not know what the right one was doing. During the mehfil, she turned her attention on a particular British officer who was immediately charmed by her. When he came out of the club to meet her, Aziz-Un's trap was successfully placed. She lured him to Shamsuddin at a discrete location where he killed the officer. Thus was conveyed a message to the British that the revolt had reached their doorstep.

The love story of Aziz-Un and Shamsuddin was the talk of the town. Shamsuddin was a brave man who was open about his visits to the kotha; Aziz-Un was also very straightforward and never hid her feelings. While they loved each other, they became soulmates only when they became part of the same revolt. It was very difficult for Aziz-Un to get even two moments of love with Shamshuddin amidst all that was transpiring. Although they knew that everything could change in a fraction of a second, if caught, they both kept making plans of their future together.

Aziz-Un also had the option of spying for the British. She could have passed on useful information in the other way which would have been more beneficial for her. The British had the power of governance, wealth and the army; she could have been on the better side of the power. But she did not choose that and instead sided with the mutineers, which made her a very courageous woman.

One day, British soldiers raided her house. This completely surprised her; she could not understand how they could enter her residence without her permission. She was traumatized by the incident and she didn't forget the humiliation that transpired that day. The British officer, who led the search raid, was actually looking for Shamshuddin. The officer had visited her kotha many a times but that day he crushed her under his heel. She felt her education, her rehearsals and her couplets which she had written after pondering over for long were all a waste. She used to live at the centre of the market and had devoted many evenings to this officer. But what did she get in return—only insult and humiliation? She understood that they were on the opposing side of the revolt but she also believed that her art was sacred. So how did this officer dare to call her a prostitute and her kotha a dirty place? She fumed with rage. This also made her wonder: *Who am I*? A mere servant of the rulers in the nation they ruled?

However, some experts believe that Aziz-Un was not a prostitute. She was termed so after 18th century. She was a cultural icon but in the prism of Victorian, moralistic middle-class reformist discourse, she was categorized as a prostitute by the British.

Nana Saheb meanwhile had reached Kanpur to boost the morale of the mutineers. While the mutiny sepoys were looking for a leader themselves, Nana Saheb had got his reasons to be against the British. It is believed that at this juncture, a meeting took place between Nana Saheb and Shamshuddin on a boat, in the middle of River Ganga. The boat had only a chosen few from both the sides. While they were in touch earlier, an agreement was now reached that Shamshuddin and his men will fight with Nana Saheb against the British government.

Some believe that Aziz-Un too was a part of this meeting.

ADRISHYA

River Ganga at Kanpur where Nana Saheb and Shamshuddin were believed to have met

Nobody knew at that time that the revolt of 1857 would become a significant historical event of the country. But everybody trusted their leaders; Aziz-Un was absolutely ready to fight alongside Nana Saheb for freedom. She even wished to don a suit of armour and jump in the war. But so far this had not happened.

Aziz-Un was an informer but she still felt that she was not doing enough. She wanted to get more actively involved in the revolt. She wanted to be a soldier; she had transformed from a delicate woman to a soldier in her passion for her country. She had left the old world of bangles, ghungroos, perfumes and beautiful dresses, and now wanted to don a suit of armour and a sword, and be accepted in the middle of the battleground, where there would be blood, dust and explosions all around. In later documents, there was a mention of Aziz-Un being right in the middle of the battlefield and also looking after the wounded, feeding and encouraging them. It is also possible that she even entertained them in the evenings. She was a very strong woman but then one day when Shamshuddin's body was brought in, she could not bear the sight of it. He had died in the bombarding by the British soldiers in their cantonment areas where a fight was ongoing. He made the ultimate sacrifice for the sake of his country.

Shamshuddin and Aziz-Un had made several promises to each other; one of them was to live together forever. They knew that death was imminent but Aziz-Un had wished to die before him. She outlived Shamshuddin but his death further strengthened her resolve to fight for the revolt.

Shamshuddin had once asked her if she was aware that in the path they had chosen, their lives were dedicated in the name of their country. Together they were mediums for each other which could help them realize their dream for the country. Shamshuddin's demise and his memory did not make her weak; instead it refreshed her aim and goal.

ADRISHYA

Image of a battlefield during the revolt

At times when the situation was tense and things around her were changing, it was also an opportunity for Aziz-Un to take up a different role. It was a rare chance that did not come calling every day. So she also changed herself, her land and her role. Aziz-Un dared to cross a territory where women were forbidden; she donned the role of a mutiny sepoy. When she first lifted the pistol, she had thought it would be very heavy. But then she also knew that nothing was heavier than the ankle-bells around her feet while she used to perform.

When we take a look at the initial stage of the revolt of 1857, it is clear that the sepoys and Nana

Saheb had taken Kanpur under their control. There were morchas and juloos (celebratory processions) around the city to celebrate this, and in such procession Aziz-Un was spotted in the dress of a sepoy, on a horse. A reference to this is found in the accounts of Travelians, Janki Prasad, Nanak Chand and also V.D. Savarkar. The reference of the same can be also found at the Archives Deposition when Col. Williams instituted an enquiry on the procession that was taken out. These clearly suggest that she was there as a part of the procession.

Aziz-Un had done everything possible in her capacity for her country. Her country was as dear to her as she was to it. She was only longing for the hour when there would be no more white people in the country who looked down upon its own people.

The revolt however was not successful and the British managed to seize power from the sepoys. On regaining their authority, the British attacked all those institutions which could pose a threat to them in the future. These also included the kothas as they thought that the courtesans had participated in the revolt and could do so again. To malign their reputation, they equated them to prostitutes, and their kothas were branded as brothels. They started a system of police inspections, health inspections and made licences mandatory for them. Dealing with the police, who would raid at their will, became a common practice after the revolt ended. Now, no honourable man would like to visit a place which could be raided by the police anytime; thus, gradually the perception of kothas and our understanding about them deteriorated over time. The courtesans lost the respect they used to command. In today's time, many of us now are not even aware that kothas used to be an integral part of our social being.

A journey that started from a kotha had reached its destination. Aziz-Un did not want to live with any regrets. She considered herself a soldier of the country and there was no stopping her.

For a long time, the contribution of women in the history of India was ignored. The major transition of their contribution got registered in the years 1970s and 1980s. Questions about the participation of women in our freedom movement started coming up only during this time. Where were the upper-class women? Or the middle-class women? Or the women from the agriculture community or the tribes? The place of women too was gradually made secure in the history of our nation. But women like Aziz-Un have always been made to stand apart from all these other women due to their lifestyle, especially their sexuality. Since their sexual choices did not fit into the so-called normal or respectable norms, such women were ignored, even more so by history.

There is no definite answer to what happened to Aziz-Un later because we have not written and preserved our history as it should have been. One version says she went away and disappeared while the other says that she was hanged. Some also say that before she was hanged her last words were 'Nana Saheb ki Jai!' Some suggest that she left the city for a few years and then came back after a while. Hence, there is no final answer as to what ultimately happened to Aziz-Un-Nisa; whether she died fighting or went away somewhere, no one knows for sure.

EXPERTS

Lata Singh is a lecturer with the Department of History at Maitreyi College, University of Delhi. She is well known for her research on kotha and tawaif culture.

Tripurari Sharma is a playwright and director working at National School of Drama, New Delhi. She has written and directed a play on Azis-Un, titled *San Sattavan Ka Kissa*.

7
Durga Bhabhi
The Revolutionary Spy
(1907–99)

Married to a revolutionary at the age of eleven, Durga Devi Vohra was raised in an atmosphere that professed self-reliance, active rebellion and resistance to the British government in every manner possible. Wife of Bhagwaticharan Vohra, who was an active member in the freedom struggle along with Bhagat Singh, Chandrashekhar Azad, Sukhdev and Rajguru in regrouping the Hindustan Republican Army as Hindustan Socialist Republican Army (HSRA), Durga Bhabhi was involved in the planning and execution of several of HSRA's activities. One of the few women who were the

DURGA BHABHI

core members of this group, Durga Bhabhi is best known for having travelled undercover with Bhagat Singh when the British police was on the lookout for him in relation to the murder of Saunders. With her two-year-old son in tow, Durga Bhabhi never once blinked when asked to stand up for her party members. A meticulous planner, she was one of the few HSRA members to survive—she went on to live till the ripe old age of ninety-two.

Durga was born on 7 October 1907 in Allahabad. She was probably eleven years old when she got married to Bhagwaticharan Vohra. Significantly, the year 1907 was a milestone year in the history of the freedom movement in India; it was in this year that the Congress party got split in Surat into two sections—Moderates and Extremists. Also, this was an important phase in revolutionary history as Japan, which was a very small country, had just defeated Russia in 1904–05. This encouraged Indians into believing that they too can defeat the British. This marked the beginning of unrest in India.

Bhagat Singh, Rajguru and Chandrashekhar Azad were frequent visitors to the Vohra household. They did not just talk of revolution and independence, but also were resolved to achieve these for their country. Young Durga was proud of their thoughts and ideals which shaped her growing-up years.

According to Dr Pramod Kumar Srivastava, Department of Western History, Lucknow University, Bhagwaticharan Vohra was considered one of the most intelligent amongst all the Indian freedom movement revolutionaries. He was a man of fine intellect and was very fond of reading and writing. He along with Bhagat Singh, who were one of the first revolutionaries, wrote their manifesto, *Naujavan Bharat Sabha*. Bhagwaticharan had met Bhagat Singh at a school in Lahore and they continued their association since then.

Durga, however, when she married him, was not formally educated. After their marriage Bhagwaticharan motivated her to study and at one point of time they used to go to the same school. After completing her matriculation exams, Durga also got a certificate in Prabhakar[3] and later used to teach in a small school nearby.

Bhagwaticharan was the force behind Durga's transformation from a student into a teacher. She

---

[3]Prabhakar degree is a degree given in the field of music. It is better known as Sangeet Prabhakar.

understood the importance of education and believed that children would one day grow up to lay the foundation of independent India. Very soon, she started teaching other children—at the school in the mornings and at home in the evenings. Her home in the evenings would be full of children from the neighbourhood, their laughter and shrieks creating a general racket. One of these kids was her own son, Sachi. The Vohra household generally used to be either bumbling with the chorus of kids or the whisper of revolutionaries.

Bhagwaticharan and Durga's house was not just a house, but a hub of political activities and revolutionary thoughts. It was a new kind of a house—several revolutionaries inspired by different ideologies used to come there; exchange of thoughts and ideas used to take place here from which, at times, rose the foundation of a new ideology. Their path to freedom—which was revolutionary in nature—was quite different from Mahatma Gandhi's ideology.

The most important job during those turbulent days was of passing information. Revolutionary comrades could not meet each other every day as that would have led to suspicion. Then one day, Bhagwaticharan handed a revolver to Durga. She was surprised. Who gives a pistol to the mother of his child? But then she realized that he probably had anticipated the danger lurking at the corner and thus had given the revolver to her for self-defence.

Perhaps also because she was a housewife, a mother and a teacher, she was not likely to be suspected. As a young girl in her twenties it was hard to imagine then that she could be passing information or carrying explosives from one place to other. That's the reason she was entrusted with the job of spying. Now, there was not a corner left in her house where some or the other work related to the movement was not going on. While other housewives were busy cooking meals, she with her husband and his group were making plans to achieve the country's independence.

In 1925, Sachindra Nath Sanyal, author of *Bandijeevan* (Life in Captivity), founded the Hindustan Republican Army (HRA) and wrote its manifesto, *The Revolutionary*. This manifesto was quietly pasted at various places by the revolutionaries on 1 January 1925. This group was not interested in only throwing the British out of the country; rather they emphasized the reasons of why they wanted the British to leave. There was unequal treatment, poverty, exploitation, drainage of resources and inequality in Indians vis-à-vis their imperial rulers; they believed that unless the British left India, they could not construct a revolutionary and ideal society.

THE REVOLUTIONARY

Number: 1st, Issue: 1st and Date: 1 January 1925

"Chaos is necessary to the birth of a new star" and the birth of life is accompanied by agony and pain. India is also taking a new birth and is passing through that inevitable phase, when chaos and agony shall play their destined role, when all calculations shall prove futile, when the wise and the mighty shall be bewildered by the simple and the week, when great empires shall crumble down and new nations shall arise and surprise humanity with the splendour and glory which shall be all its own.

This new power, which is shaking the world from its very depths, this new spirit which is working miracles behind the scene, is also manifesting itself in the young blood of India and is taking the shape of a movement which is despised and ignored by the wise and the learned, and is being described as the wild dreams of a few mad men. This remarkable movement is the revolutionary movement in young India.

The revolutionary movement has unnerved the weak, has inspired the robust and healthy, and has confounded the worldly wise and the learned. This movement can never be crushed just as much as the coming of the spring can never be thwarted. It will never die out until it has fulfilled the mission for which it has taken its birth.

An image of the first issue of *The Revolutionary*

A member of the party, young Inder used to help Durga with her chores often. Sometimes he would make tea, get things for her and do all kinds of odd jobs to help her. One day Inder and Durga were given some bills. Durga was expected to distribute them among people while Inder had to stick them on walls.

Inder had planned to meet Durga Bhabhi at her

home after sticking the posters. However, while he was distributing notices at a junction in the middle of the city, Inder unknowingly went to the road next to the police station to stick the posters and was spotted by the police. A fast runner, Inder tried to run but they shot him in the leg and he died. Durga and her comrades had earlier vowed never to shed a tear on anybody's death, as it disrespected the sacrifice of the martyr. The bullet hit Inder but its poison was gently getting dissolved in everyone's blood in the form of revenge.

This is what being a revolutionary meant at that time—the constant danger, the threat to life, the work of a spy. Initially, Durga Bhabhi's role was to collect information and to make secret codes which were also known as revolutionary codes. If she wrote a letter, sometime some lines were written in milk, so that they could only be read against the light or with the help of a candle. She also used to help in the distribution of letters. In a way, she used to work like a postbox, and at times she even used to call herself that—a postbox!

In 1928, the revolutionaries from Bengal, Rajasthan, Uttar Pradesh and Punjab met and revived the HRA as Hindustan Socialist Republican Association/Army

(HSRA).[4] 'Socialism' was the new addition to their ideology and it was resolved that the aim was to create a socialist country. That same year, Simon Commission, led by Sir John Simon, arrived in India with an aim to look into necessary reforms in the constitution. As there was no Indian representative in the commission, the Congress and other political parties opposed it as the high-handed attitude of the British. On his journey across India, Simon met severe protests with slogans like 'Simon, Go Back' ringing the air. When the commission reached Lahore, it was opposed there as well, under the leadership of Lala Lajpat Rai. As the huge crowd gathered became more and more unrelenting, the police started a lathicharge, in which Lalaji was grievously injured, succumbing to death very soon.

Everyone was shocked by the cruel death of Lalaji. They wondered how many more would need to sacrifice themselves for the cause. For how long would they watch their loved ones getting martyred? After all, everyone who died was a child to a mother, an idol of a young

---

[4]The Kakori train robbery incident of 1925 had been executed by HRA members but after the arrest and subsequent execution of four of its leaders—Ashfaqullah Khan, Ram Prasad Bismil, Roshan Singh and Rajendra Lahiri—the HRA was dealt a severe blow, and was inactive for a few years.

man and an inspiration to an organization. Questions were many but no one had any answer. It was Durga Bhabhi who broke the silence. It was time to revive the old Hindi proverb—*'Jiski lathi, uska sar'* (a person who carries a stick to hit others, must be hit back with his own stick). She said that to avenge Lalaji's death, they must kill the English officer James A. Scott, superintendent of police, who had given the order of lathicharge. Bhagwaticharan, Bhagat Singh, Rajguru and Sukhdev decided unanimously that they would avenge this death which they considered was an insult to their country. They vowed that they would not let Scott go unpunished. Bhagat Singh agreed with her and took it upon himself to execute the act.

They hatched a plan for his assassination. On the designated day, John P. Saunders, an assistant superintendent of police, came on a motorcycle and Scott came in a car and in a case of mistaken identity, Saunders got killed, instead of Scott.

Bhagwaticharan was then in Calcutta for an urgent work. Durga Bhabhi was alone at home when she heard the news of the killing of Saunders on the radio. The news also said that the police knew who was behind his murder, and they would soon be captured.

The British had a reference of one of the killers:

that the man had a short beard and he was a sardar. This was Bhagat Singh. After the incident, he shaved his beard off and got his hair cropped. He looked like a new man now—very fair and handsome.

Durga started oscillating in fear, patience, hope and hopelessness. One day, while she was teaching the kids, she heard a knock on her door. She wondered who it could be at that time of the evening. She opened the door to see an English-looking man standing there. She was relieved when she saw Azad and Sukhdev also behind him. The man entered her house confidently and smiling. She was bewildered as to who he was and how he could enter her house like that. She took Sukhdev aside and asked him about the man's identity. Sukhdev laughed, as did the Englishman. He said that if Durga Bhabhi could not recognize him that meant he had passed the test. That man was Bhagat Singh!

The happiness of seeing her comrade did not last long as they told her that the police was looking for them desperately. Durga immediately wrote an application to the principal of her school and requested leave for a few days. She knew that if nothing was done, they would soon be caught and killed. Something needed to be done fast. She sent her students home, who were happy to get unexpected holidays. She smiled looking at their innocent faces whose lives were not marked by the intricacies of the revolution. She hatched a plan to leave Lahore for Calcutta that very night on a train. Her comrades also agreed to it.

Durga Devi was a leader. Men used to discuss issues with her and take her advice. Bhagat Singh respected her enormously, and it was a relationship of mutual cordiality. She was an important member of the group. The fact that these revolutionaries took a great risk of travelling with Durga Devi indicated that they trusted her completely.

Durga's heart was racing with anxiety but she knew that it was important to save Bhagat Singh, Sukhdev and Rajguru from the police. Calcutta, as it was so far from Lahore, seemed like a safe haven. She felt their lives were more important than hers or her son Sachi's. Both Bhagat Singh and Sukhdev warned her about the possible dangers if caught. They could all be killed, including toddler Sachi. She replied that Sachi was the son of a revolutionary and if he got to die as a martyr that would be a privilege. Such was Durga Devi's dedication and commitment to her country that she was willing to sacrifice her little child which was almost sure to happen.

It is important to note that at that time women were

usually working in the capacity of wives to revolutionaries in such organizations. But in this episode, Durga Bhabhi changed her traditional role of a wife. She pretended to be the wife of Bhagat Singh in this journey to Calcutta. She wore an expensive silk sari, and Bhagat Singh was dressed as a gentleman. They booked two first-class tickets; Rajguru, who was pretending to be the servant, got a ticket for the third class. Chandra Shekhar Azad was also there in the disguise of a sage.

It was almost impossible to leave Lahore at that time. Everybody knew that the people who had executed the assassination would try to leave Lahore via the bus stand or the train station. The British police were hunting for them; they were waiting for them to leave Lahore.

At the first opportunity, Azad, who was sitting on a bench at the platform disguised as a sage, too, climbed inside the train. They were all carrying weapons because they knew that the escape won't be easy. They were expecting an encounter at the station. The security was so strong at the station that not even a bird could have flapped its wing without getting noticed. They were wearing expensive clothes but they were ready to die. Gathering their wits, they got inside the train. Once they were inside, Durga was somewhat relieved. But she was wrong. A British officer had noticed the group and he climbed into the train after them. Durga and Bhagat Singh had not even settled when the officer entered their coupe. Before he could say a thing, Durga Bhabhi handed the crying Sachi to him, asking him to hold. The officer got confused. He was not ready for this. He quickly handed Sachi back to Durga and left the coupe. He must have thought that no woman would carry a child so small with her if she was on a secret mission.

The train left Lahore station. A day when not even a bird could have escaped from there, Durga Bhabhi managed to get Bhagat Singh, Rajguru and Azad safely out of Lahore. She managed to escape with the three most wanted revolutionaries right under the nose of the British police. No matter how famous and important these revolutionaries were, for her, at times, they were like her son Sachi.

Bhagwaticharan and his sister, Sushila, came to the station once the group reached Calcutta. Later, Sushila, better known as Didi, took them to Seth Chhaju Ram who was a rich businessman of the city and a sympathizer to the freedom cause. They met other revolutionaries too—for example, Jatindra Nath Das, a leading revolutionary of Bengal, who taught them the method of making bombs. It was a complete change for them in Calcutta. Bhagat Singh stayed there for sometime while Durga Bhabhi returned to Lahore after a few days.

On 8 April 1929, Bhagat Singh and Batukeshwar Dutt hurled bombs in the Central Legislative Assembly in Delhi and shouted slogans of 'Inquilaab Zindabad'. Subsequently, they were arrested. Bhagwaticharan and Durga Bhabhi meanwhile were back in Lahore for sometime now after their tryst in Calcutta. They were building up the process of making bombs at their home which was coming along fairly well. In a bid to free Bhagat Singh, they now planned to bomb the jail where he was being imprisoned.

Now, there were two jails in Lahore. One was the Central Jail and the other was Borstal Jail. Both the jails were opposite each other. The court proceedings were being held inside the jail. Everyday Bhagat Singh was moved from one jail to another. The plan was to bomb when Bhagat Singh was being moved between the jails. For this, they needed to make bombs and then test these. Ultimately, the bombs got ready.

On 28 May 1930, the group decided to test the bombs. To mark this as an auspicious occasion, Durga Bhabhi put a tilak on her husband's forehead and gave him a sweet to eat. Her porch was full of squealing children who also wanted sweets, but she told them that they would get the sweets once her husband and the others would come back. The children agreed. Bhagwaticharan and his comrades left the house to test the bombs near the river. Not just Durga, but the kids also kept looking at the door to see when the men would come back. Everyone was waiting for their return.

When the group reached the river, they got on to test the bombs. However, they noticed that the trigger of one of the bombs was loose. Rajguru said he would test it but Bhagwaticharan stopped him, saying he would do it himself. He was the expert in the group. But when he threw the bomb to test it, due to the loose trigger it blasted in his hands. His hand got blown off from the explosion, his intestines burst out of his stomach and he fell down unconscious. Yashpal and Vaishampayan, his other comrades, ran to the site and saw the body of Bhagwaticharan. They could not have burnt the body; so they immersed the remains in the river.

The bigger task now was to inform Durga Bhabhi of the tragic mishap. The kids heard the footsteps before Durga Devi did. They ran up to her, asking for the sweets as was promised. She gave sweets to all. But one look at the men and she knew something was very wrong. Vaishampayan and Yashpal could not look her in the eye and she was only searching for her husband. But he was not there. The hung heads and apologetic eyes ultimately gave it away. She understood that her husband was never coming back home.

Bhagwaticharan Vohra's martyrdom was unexpected. The plan was to free Bhagat Singh. Before they could even attempt to free Bhagat Singh, they lost Bhagwaticharan to the accident. It wasn't just a loss to the organization or the nation; it was a huge personal loss to Durga Bhabhi.

In 1930, after her husband's death, Durga Bhabhi left Lahore and became a revolutionary on the run which resulted in several travels in numerous disguises. She could change into any disguise when the need arose. When she went to Rawalpindi, she stayed with a group dressed in salwar kameez. She came back to Lahore carrying bombs in a tattered mat. When she was in Jaipur, she was dressed in a lehanga like the locals. She even went to meet Bhagat Singh in the jail as his aunt. He had tears in his eyes but she stood strong. She used to regularly go to the jail to meet him and give him information on the workings of the party.

Bhagwaticharan was not there anymore but his dream for his country continued to motivate Durga Bhabhi. She also had to bring up their son. She was the party's spy and continued her contribution.

Earlier the revolutionaries, including Durga Bhabhi, had planned to get Bhagat Singh freed from the jail. But after Bhagwaticharan's death that possibility was no longer there. His trial was national news and the whole country was keeping a watch. A horde of people used to collect outside the jail to hear the case. Finally, Bhagat Singh, Rajguru and Sukhdev were sentenced to death by hanging on 7 October 1930. It was Durga Devi who insisted that something must be done. She hatched a plan to go to Bombay and avenge the death sentence of Bhagat Singh and Sukhdev by shooting the Governor of Punjab (Sir) Geoffrey de Montmorency who was in the city at that time. She had the support of fellow revolutionaries Vaishampayan and Yashpal. Azad, however, was not in favour of it. He was emotionally devastated at the loss of Bhagwaticharan and other fellow comrades but did not support Durga Bhabhi, Vaishampayan and Yashpal going to Bombay and doing something in retaliation, in which they could even get killed. He wanted them to have patience and not do anything in haste. But the trio insisted on giving a befitting reply and went to Bombay anyway. Their motive was to shoot the governor of Bombay.

When they tried to find a way to enter the Governor House, they found that it was impossible to get in. There was strict security outside the house but Durga Bhabhi and the others did not want to return without doing anything. After waiting for long hours, they saw some British police officers coming out of the house on Lamington Road. Her comrades ordered Durga Bhabhi to shoot, and she shot an officer.

However, while getting down from the car in which they were escaping, Durga Bhabhi's sari got stuck in the door and tore. After the incident, when the police were investigating, they recovered the torn piece and realized that a woman was involved in the killing. As there were not too many women participating in the freedom movement, the police knew that it would not be too difficult to trace the perpetrator. The British press acknowledged this incident as the first ever woman terrorist attack and so did history books in later times.

Durga Devi took shelter at the residence of other revolutionaries in Bombay but the police zeroed in on her location and came knocking on the doors of the house where she was staying. On the arrival of the police, she immediately went to bed, pretending to be an old ailing woman. But her son Sachi was playing outside. When the police asked about him, the owner of the house said he was his sister's son. Had the police officer asked Sachi where he had come from, he would have definitely told him the truth. The game of hide-and-seek that Durga Devi was playing with the British was becoming dangerous with each passing day.

Durga Bhabhi was left with no one of her own—neither her husband nor her comrades like Bhagat Singh or Azad. While Bhagat Singh, Sukhdev and Rajguru were hanged on 23 March 1931, Chandra Shekhar Azad too was killed in an encounter almost a month earlier (27 February) in Allahabad. No one was there to support such a revolutionary woman. To make matters worse, the police too was looking for her and with young Sachi she didn't know where to go next. She was torn in her conscience. She had not accepted defeat but she needed some time to think about the future. The question in her mind was—what next?

Handing over her son to her trusted ones, she left on another journey, this time absolutely alone—the journey of a rebel.

Durga Bhabhi had played every role in her life with

DURGA BHABHI

perfection—as a wife in managing the household and a sister-in-law for all her revolutionary brothers. She had even played a spy and had been a true patriot to her country but she wondered why she failed as a mother. She wondered why she had to choose between her son and the revolution. The police was neither able to get hold of her nor was it leaving her in peace. Tired and frustrated, she surrendered. She was sentenced to three years in jail for her role in the killing of the British officer in Bombay.

In jail, Durga Devi used to recall what Bhagat Singh had told her—that it was better to achieve martyrdom at a young age than dying in old age, withered and wrinkled. They all had tried their best, but she felt that martyrdom came only to a chosen few.

Durga Devi was the first-generation woman revolutionary in Indian politics at that time. There was no woman revolutionary before her, except Madam Kama, who had designed the tricolour. After her there was only Durga Devi.

Having spent three years in jail, Durga Bhabhi, after her release, went and settled in Lucknow. Having spent her life teaching children, in Lucknow too she gathered four children and started teaching them. She opened a little school in a rented house next to the Lucknow Publishing House. Gradually, the school got bigger, and India also got its independence. Durga Bhabhi then opened a trust in Lucknow, called the Rafi Ahmad Memorial Trust, and established the Lucknow Montessori Inter-College, with Acharya Narendra Dev as its first president. It was evident that the objective of Durga Devi Vohra was not limited to only securing freedom for India. She also wanted to help construct a new nation and she knew that it was only possible through education.

A woman with extraordinary strength and moral character, Durga Bhabhi hoped to build a new India despite losing all her loved ones.

She had moved on from being a spy to a teacher.

EXPERTS

Dr Nonica Dutta is an associate professor of Modern History, University of Delhi.

Dr Pramod Kumar Srivastava is a reader in the Department of Western History, Lucknow University. He is a renowned historian and writer who has penned many works on HSRA, its members and their contribution to the freedom movement of India.

8

Noor Inayat Khan

The Unlikely Spy
(1914–44)

A Sufi poet, a princess by birth and a children's author, Noor Inayat Khan grew up in the midst of the growing Sufi movement in Europe. Her father, Inayat Khan Rehmat Khan Pathan, was the founder of the Sufi Order in the West in 1914 and was a teacher of Universal Sufism. But as World War II drew closer, reaching the doorsteps of her Parisian home, Noor and her brother, brought up to pursue the path of non-violence, were now faced with a choice: to stand by and watch as the world fell into pieces or join the forces fighting for justice. Guided by her convictions, Noor walked into the most dangerous post in all of Paris—that of the sole link between the rebel groups of France and their support system in England. Running an entire circuit all by herself, the Sufi princess, a misfit in the army and a most unlikely secret agent, grew into one of the bravest Special Operations Executive (SOE) members. She even went on to win posthumously the George Cross—the highest gallantry award for civilians by the Government of United Kingdom.

Noor Inayat Khan was a descendant of Tipu Sultan—the king of Mysore—who was killed by the British in 1799. Her father Inayat Khan belonged to a noble Indian Muslim family—his mother was a descendant of the uncle of Tipu Sultan. Noor's mother, Aura Baker, was British but was born and brought up in America. Aura met Inayat Khan during a Sufi lecture in America and they both fell deeply in love with each other. They got married in 1913 and the same year, Noor Inayat Khan was born.

A portrait of Tipu Sultan

Germany invaded France on 10 May 1940. The war lasted six weeks and Paris surrendered to Germany on 14 June without firing a single bullet. France got a new president, Marshal Petain, who was forty-eight years old and had fought in World War I. On 22 June 1940, he signed a treaty to end the war with Hitler at the Forest of Compiegne. This was a place of historic significance as at the end of World War I in 1918, Germany had accepted defeat from France at this very place.

When Paris got invaded, Noor and her brother

Vilayat had to reach a decision. They were not sure if they should stay at Fazal Manzil, their home in Paris, anymore. They finally decided that even though they were Sufis, who believed in non-violence, it would be wrong to just sit and let the enemy occupy their country. Noor and her family decided to leave their home in Paris and move to London before the Germans could reach the city.

Noor Inayat Khan's father had spent all his life travelling in Moscow, London and France but he took his last breath in India. There were days when she used to miss him a lot. He was a man of many stories. Though she did not have her father with her anymore, she had his stories, Indian stories. Noor had even made a collection of short stories for children and had got it published as a book. She wanted to become a writer. But with the defeat of France her life took such a sudden turn that she folded her dreams and aspirations and decided to take a different course.

Fazal Manzil had been their home for a long time; Noor's father always used to tell them that they were the descendants of Tipu Sultan and they should have a strong grounding morally, and not be attached to material possessions. However, when she left her home in Paris for London, she left her heart in France. Little did she know though that soon she would be back. Both the siblings decided that once in England they would volunteer in the war efforts and as a duty would fight fascism, Nazism and the German occupation.

Noor reached London but it was the time of the Blitz. London was burning and the country was in shambles. At times it appeared that London too would give up and surrender to the Germans. Londoners were scared and carried a feeling of desolation in their eyes.

The Blitz started on 7 September 1940 in London when German planes started dropping bombs on the city. This gruesome act continued for seventy-six nights. The people of London often had to take shelter in underground train stations to save themselves. The British government was in desperate need of people in the armed forces. All over the city there were posters requesting citizens to join the army. It was during this time that Noor Inayat Khan decided to apply to the Women's Auxiliary Air Force (WAAF).

Noor's first application, however, got rejected. The reasons were numerous—she was a French citizen, born in Moscow and had an Indian name. But Noor had made up her mind. She questioned the authority; how could they not consider her British when she had a British mother and carried a British protected person's passport. The reply was immediate with a confirmation of interview.

London, during the Blitz, World War II

Noor hailed from a political family; she was also quite well-informed about the political developments in India. She was aware of the ongoing Quit India Movement in India where all major leaders—Gandhi and Nehru included—had been arrested. Her interview got interesting when she was asked if she would support those leaders in India who are opposed to the British. Noor gave a quick reply, 'At this moment,' she said, 'when the war is on and the fight is on against fascism, when we are having such an important battle against fascism, at this moment I would support the British. But the moment the war is over I will support Indian Independence.' The British officials were stunned by her reply. Noor's father used to tell her that it was never wrong to say the truth and that is what she did; she spoke frankly, without any hesitation. They were left shocked but Noor still made through the WAAF.

Noor now carried a badge on her chest. From Noor Inayat Khan she had become Nora Baker. But then there were numerous other names to follow in the years to come—Noor, Nora or the secret agent Madeleine. It was the first time in her life that she became a number: Aircraft's Woman Number# something. She had a hat and a WAAF uniform and she actually loved it. In a way, she had achieved a kind of freedom from the over-protected home environment that she was brought up in where she was Babuli or Peerzadi Noor Inayat Khan, the eldest child of Hazrat Inayat Khan. She was happy to be free of carrying the family name. She was happy to be anonymous, to be just a number. She was glad to be one of the many young girls who were working forward for a cause. The thought made her ecstatic.

During the training she met officer Leo Marx who was their instructor. He was a patient teacher and was known to calmly answer every question. Noor was selected for the training of a wireless operator. She was also taught plotting and Morse Code. It was a completely new experience for her. For the first time in her life she felt that she was doing something substantial that could achieve some change in the turbulent world that she lived in.

Women who were members of the WAAF used to do a variety of jobs. Noor worked as a barrage balloon girl. These were people whose job was to manage the big hot air balloons which were erected to protect the army headquarters and establishments from enemy bombardment. These women were plotters too who would plot the location of the German army. Some of them were even trained to be wireless operators.

Noor wrote a letter to her mother to tell her about

her new life. She wrote in detail about her daily routine. She wrote that she felt that if Indians like her would support the British in World War II—join their army of other services—then, in return, they would be obliged to give India its independence. Her father would have agreed with her view.

Soon after her WAAF training, Noor was called for an interview with SOE. The SOE was set up by the British government to conduct espionage, sabotage and reconnaissance in occupied Europe (and later, also in occupied Southeast Asia) against the Axis powers and to aid local resistance movements. It was an initiative by London with the aim that when America and Britain would join hands to fight together, there should be intelligence providers spread over all those countries which had been occupied. The SOE was an extremely important and secret agency. Noor was the only one chosen amongst her team for this interview.

During the SOE interview, Noor was asked if she was to be sent to Paris as an undercover agent, would she be willing to go. It was a dangerous mission but her answer was a quick yes. In the small interview room of SEO, Noor was told that she was going to be recruited and sent to France on a secret mission. She would not get a uniform to wear; so the usual protection of a uniform was non-existent. She was to go there as an agent and if caught by the enemy, there was no way she could be released because there was no prisoner of war policy or Geneva Convention for secret agents. Spies were only shot. Despite knowing what she was getting into, Noor said yes, she would go.

During her SOE training, Noor and other girls like her were taught to send and receive code messages. Those messages were coded and decoded by the agents themselves. That meant creating a key or a password to decode every message. It was a new language for her where instead of letters dashes and dots were used. She made a code key out of a poem she had written. She found it entertaining, though it wasn't easy. The writer within her had found out a way to write messages in a new language.

The selected members underwent different training sessions. As part of the initial training, they were taught the use of weapons, a bit of Morse Code and some physical exercises. Once they cleared that, those selected were sent to a school in Scotland where they were given paramilitary training which taught them to survive under any condition. From there they were sent to the Ringway Airport, Manchester, and then to the north-western region of England where they were given parachute training so that if and when the time would come, they could jump off from aeroplanes. For the last leg of the training, they were given some more lessons on wireless and then they were finally appointed as agents. In the course of the training, many a times they were subjected to mock interrogations so that they could realize what it might be like to live in an occupied country.

It was important to control one's fear while fighting the Gestapo. But during the training sessions of the mock Gestapo raids, Noor would be so shattered that her training officers felt that if she were ever to face the actual Gestapo she would stand no chance before them. As much as Noor wanted to clear the test, she knew she would fail in the assessment.

Noor's instructors gave her adverse reports. One of them went on to say that her attitude was not suitable for the job. Another one wrote that she was scared of weapons and she did not want to kill anyone under any circumstances; maybe she was sceptical about the usage of weapons. Her officers considered her weak and scared. They were not entirely wrong, but they were not entirely right either. She was weak and scared but she was not a traitor. And she was ready to prove it to them if ever such a time came. She was lost, but she was looking for freedom.

Noor was an unlikely spy. She found it difficult to lie because her father had always told her that she was a Sufi and so should not lie. The problem was that it was going to conflict with her work. As a spy she had a false identity, false papers and basically she had to take the cover of lies to maintain her status of an agent. She was fine with that; it was just that she could never lie face-to-face.

Despite all her flaws, Leo Marx gave her another chance. He asked her to create a message of two hundred and fifty characters. She was quick in creating the message but in her nervousness she started correcting it. She was unsure how he would take her message; so she tried to write and rewrite the message several times. Finally, she showed him the message and waited for his response. Marx then explained to her the mistakes in an unusual way. He was himself an amateur writer and he explained things to her from a writer's point of view.

Leo Marx was very patient with Noor. He was aware that she was a descendant of a princely family and could have her family ideals—she would never lie. The challenge lay in how she would make a good agent despite her reluctance to lie. He was requested to handle her carefully during her training. Leo picked up her book on children. There was a story about monkeys in it where the leader of a pack of monkeys lay between the peaks of two mountains to bridge the gap and asked his army to climb over him to go over to the other side. Thus he saved the lives of eighty thousand monkeys. Leo said that her codes are that bridge and if she ever makes a mistake with them she would be putting somebody's life in danger. Noor understood that she had to become that monkey who sacrificed himself for the mission and resolved never to send a wrong code. Leo also told her to never send a code of eighteen characters from her machine. It would work as a signal and if he ever gets a code of eighteen characters from her machine, he would understand that she is in trouble.

When Noor went to the field, her messages were as she had resolved to do; always precise, correct and with no mistakes. The officers were impressed with her. Finally, in June 1943, the day came when she had to journey back to Paris; she was happy going back to the city of her childhood. Her destination was 40, Rue Erlanger, Paris.

Noor was allowed to carry only one pistol, few French francs and a map of Paris. The agents used to travel in a night flight. The night plane Noor travelled in was a small plane called Lysander. It used to take the agents on a full-moon night because then the pilot could clearly see the landing field without the help of spotlights. Noor flew to Paris on one such night. As the flight descended, there was a group of people who stood in an L-shape on the field with flares in their hands which they flashed in Morse Code. This was the indicator to the pilot for landing. Evidently, it was very dangerous: a plane landing on an unlit field and the secret agents filing out in the dark. After the landing, the agents were given a cycle and a map, and they were on their own.

Noor reached the address she had been given; she had been instructed to meet an old lady there. But a young man named Gary opened the door for her. He invited her in and introduced her to his sister Rene. Gary and Rene were members of the French Resistance who worked in coordination with British spies.

The Resistance had started brewing in France and initially people stood up against the establishment individually but with passing time they soon formed small groups and resisted against the German government in whichever way they knew. These groups used to print newspapers and leaflets and distribute them. A while later, this movement shook the very roots of Germany. The British Broadcasting Company (BBC) also played a vital role. America soon joined hands with the British, around December 1941, and made the French Resistance against Germany stronger.

Gary and Rene updated Noor about everything that was happening in France at that time. One day, during one BBC programme, wireless decoders decoded a message which read that 'Tonight Jasmine will play the flute' on the radio. It was a message for the operatives of the British army that Noor and the other agents had reached France.

Meanwhile, Gary and Rene became good friends with Noor. Gary gave her the code name 'Madeleine'. Noor got the kind of emotional support from Gary and Rene that kept her sane in Paris.

The F-section of the SOE had many circuits (operative groups). Every circuit was manned by an organizer—a wireless operator—who was usually a man but later women too stepped in and worked as couriers as well. In 1943, Prosper Circuit was the biggest group in Paris. Its operators were spread over a very large area. However, due to its sheer number, it was inevitable that some of them would get caught by the Gestapo sooner or later, and this was exactly what happened on 24 June 1943. It had not even been a week since Noor had arrived in Paris.

By July there was only one transmitter left in Paris—

Noor's. A sense of danger always surrounded her but she did not have the time to be scared. It was she who informed Leo Marx about the end of Prosper Circuit. He asked her to return to London immediately. But Noor refused; she had just arrived in Paris, and she knew she was the only wireless operator left in the city. She told Leo that she would help him build another circuit. Leo agreed but he knew that Noor was putting herself in grave danger—the danger of being captured by the dreaded Gestapo. This was indeed very brave of her and tells us a lot about her character and her upbringing. Noor was exemplarily courageous.

Between July and October Noor worked as hard as six operators together. She was the only operator left in Paris. The Germans had to detect the transmissions of only a single operator to initiate a crackdown. She was getting deeper into dangerous territories with every passing day and the noose of the Gestapo was tightening around her neck. Still, London would wait for her messages at 15:00 GMT (three in the afternoon) every day as Noor continued in her dangerous mission of opposing fascist forces.

Noor was aware that the German counter-intelligence agencies, Abwehr and Gestapo, knew about her existence. They knew that her code name was

Madeleine. They were also aware that it was a woman operator. Noor decided to change her appearance to avoid detection. She first dyed her hair red and then blonde.

The wireless operators were advised to not send any transmission of more than fifteen minutes. This was so because the Germans had direction-finding machines which could locate wireless sets. If the transmission exceeded fifteen to twenty minutes, they could identify and arrest the operator. Gestapo had such a machine with which they could trace an operator immediately after a transmission. To circumvent this, Noor used to take her transmission machine and go to a park after every transmission.

As a wireless operator, Noor had one of the most dangerous jobs during the war. Managing the logistical part of the job in itself was so risky; she had to carry the transmitting machine in a briefcase which weighed around fifteen kilos, and she used to travel across the city like that. She could be stopped by the authorities anywhere and questioned about what the briefcase contained; if the wireless set was detected, she could even be shot for espionage.

One day, she had just come and sat in the park when two policemen approached her and asked her about the briefcase. Noor did not want to lie. The name of her circuit was Cinema, and she told the policemen as much, that she had cinema in the briefcase and they can check if they wish. She even offered to open the briefcase to show it to them. Seeing her confidence, they let her go.

Through her transmission, Noor used to organize arm drops from London and the channelling of finances to the French Resistance. She would mark X on possible meeting spots for her meetings with people in order to hand over the money to them. She was acting both as a courier and as a radio operator. The life expectancy of radio operators was just six weeks from the time they took an assignment. London was losing all operators rapidly and Noor was the only female radio operator in the field.

One day, Noor went to meet Zheal. Zheal was the courier of Noor's circuit and she hadn't heard from him in a while. He had never missed a single meeting till then. When the wait had gotten too long, Noor was worried for him. Concerned, she had called him. Zheal had picked up the phone; his voice had sounded a bit different but Noor at that time did not register the change. Unwilling to talk on the phone for too long, he had then asked Noor to meet him at a new place and at a new time. Noor agreed to comply and went to meet Zheal at the appointed place. Little did she know that it was a trap set by the Nazi officers to capture her.

Noor ran. When she knew it was a trap laid by Zheal, she ran as fast as her legs could carry her. She was a fast runner and knew all the inner roads of Paris as well; so she could manage to outrun her followers and escape. However, the Gestapo had seen Noor's face. She knew it was time for her to leave Paris. Leo too instructed her to return to London immediately. As soon as she reached home, she gave the news of her imminent departure to Gary and Rene. She had nobody else to share the news with in Paris. Gary confessed that he and his sister would miss Noor a lot.

But disaster struck soon. One evening, after entering her home, she was attacked by an assailant who was waiting for her to come in. Noor was however trained to combat; she kicked and bit and fought her attacker with all her might. She was so fierce that he could not manage to hold her on his own. He finally fished out his pistol and pointing it at her head dialled headquarters and asked for more men. When the Gestapo arrived with more numbers, only then could they arrest Noor.

Noor was not afraid of being captured. But what shattered her was that it was Rene, Gary's sister and her friend, who had exposed her to the Gestapo for just one thousand francs. Rene, however, was shortchanged; she did not realize that she could have sold Noor to the Gestapo for more than one hundred thousand francs. It is believed that she was jealous that Noor and her brother Gary used to spend so much time together. However, there is this other possibility that Noor was friendly with an SOE agent, Frans Antin, who was once in a relationship with Rene and so a jealous Rene informed the Gestapo about her.

Little was expected from men who had forgotten how it was to be human beings. They beat her like animals.

Noor was taken and kept at 84, Avenue Foch, Paris. There were many SOE agents held there. It was a five-storey, huge and beautiful building. The agents were interrogated and tortured on the fifth floor. They wanted the code key from Noor, but she refused to hand it over to them. As a result, she was beaten so much that she could not even get a night's sleep due to the pain.

Once the Germans captured an SOE agent they used to contact Britain from the transmitter set seized, posing as an SOE agent. They had Noor's code books and they started sending misleading messages to Britain.

Leo had told her before leaving that the day Britain would get a message of more than eighteen characters from her set, they would understand that she is in trouble. Noor waited for the Germans to make that mistake and they did it eventually. After a long time, the SOE headquarters realized that Noor had been captured. Unfortunately for Noor, due to the negligence of London, that message never got delivered to Leo.

When for a long time nothing worked out, Noor thought of other ways to escape. Once she got lucky to sneak out of a window but was caught. At another time, along with an SOE agent, John Star, and French resistance member Col. Fey, she cut the window bars and reached the terrace of the jail to escape. But ill fate struck her path again. The air raid siren blew at the wrong time; attendance was taken of all the inmates for a headcount and Noor and her friends were caught.

Due to her constant efforts to escape, Noor was asked to sign a declaration that she would not try to run away again. John Star signed it but Noor refused saying that as a British officer it was her duty to try to escape. Noor was then shifted to the Dachau concentration camp. She was kept alone in her cell and the very next day she was executed. It is said that the last thing which she said was 'liberty'.

There are proofs which indicate that the night she was executed, she was raped.

Before he passed away, an aged Vilayat told Shrabani Basu (author of *The Life of Noor Inayat Khan*) the following: 'I have only one regret…that as a Sufi I should forgive. But I cannot forgive one person, Rene. I cannot forgive Rene.'

EXPERTS

Dr Juliette Pattinson is a reader in History at the University of Kent and has authored *Behind Enemy Lines: Gender, Passing and the Special Operations Executive in the Second World War*.

Shrabani Basu is the author of *Spy Princess: The Life of Noor Inayat Khan*. She is also the founder of the Noor Inayat Khan Memorial Trust, London.

9

Saraswati Rajamani

Netaji's Spy
(1925–Present)

Born into a wealthy Indian family in Myanmar (formerly Burma) that actively supported the non-violent path preached by Gandhi, Saraswati (also Saraswathi) Rajamani at the age of ten decided that for India to be truly independent, force would be required and the perpetrators of injustice must be made to pay for their crimes. While her family was deeply engrossed in spreading the message of the Mahatma, Saraswati turned towards Subhash Chandra Bose, who rose as an alternative to Gandhi with his message of active resistance. At the age of sixteen, Saraswati joined the

Indian National Army (INA) and braved the stark conditions of her training, dreaming for the freedom for a country she had never stepped into. From the age of sixteen to eighteen, Saraswati worked as a boy spy, entering British camps disguised as a boy servant and passing information and ammunition to the INA. Saraswati moved to India when the INA disbanded and the country won its freedom. Saraswati, now ninety-two, lives in penury in Chennai.

Saraswati Rajamani's father was a follower of Mahatma Gandhi and loved talking about him to his daughter—tales of Gandhi when he started the Non-cooperation Movement in 1920 and the theory of ahimsa or the idea of civil disobedience through the practice of ahimsa (non-violence). India was with Gandhi at that time. Many people had left their studies, jobs and businesses to be with him.

The country was witnessing turbulent times in the wake of the revolution of the century—the Non-cooperation Movement. Adjacent to India, Rangoon, which was also termed as the London of the East, was however bustling at that time—business, people,

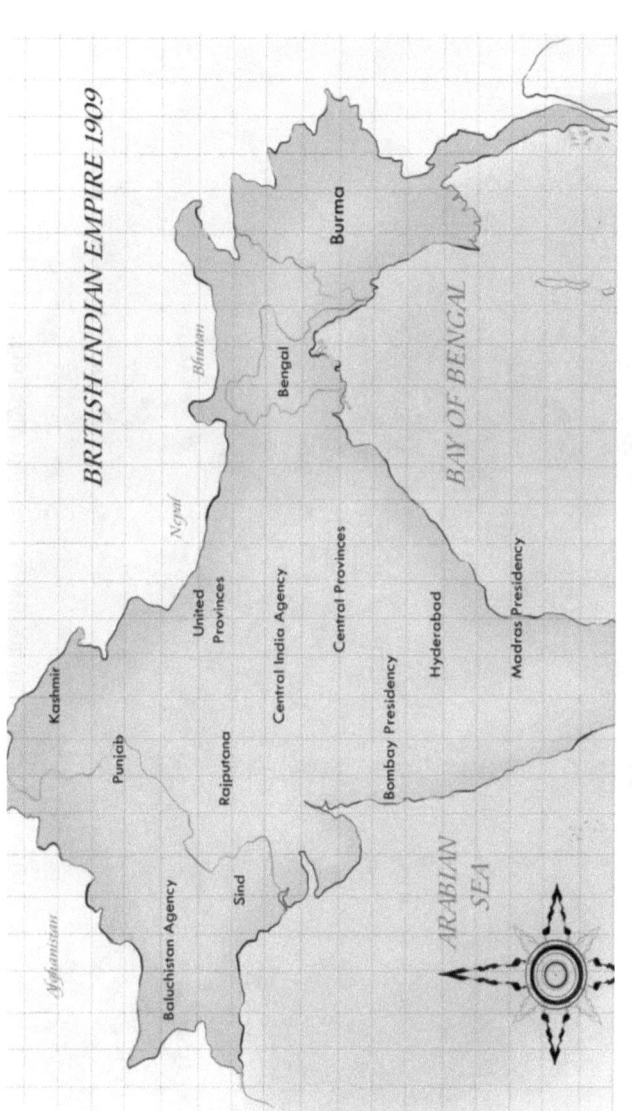

Map of British India

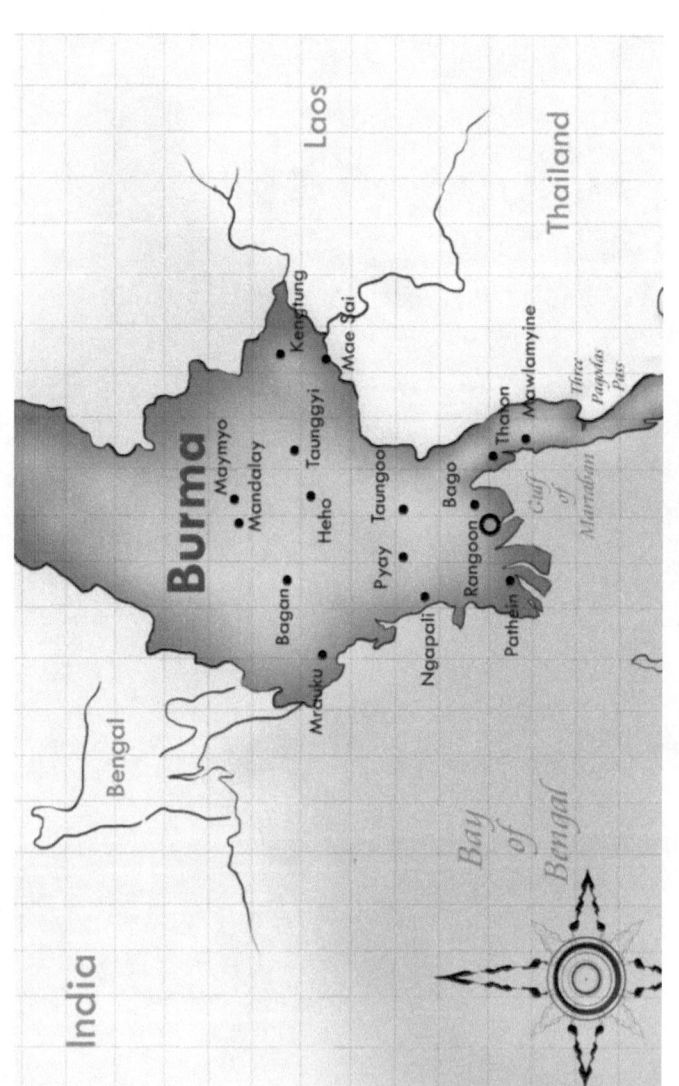

Map of Burma, later renamed Myanmar

markets, etc. The atmosphere in India was in complete contrast to that of Rangoon. Indians who wanted to work and do business used to go to Rangoon for a better life. Saraswati's father too left Tamil Nadu, in India, to settle in Rangoon.

The people of Myanmar, especially Rangoon, were emotionally attached to India. In those times, Myanmar, along with Rangoon, was a part of the erstwhile Greater India. When Myanmar got separated from India, the people living there were of the view that India should be independent too from British domination. That was one reason why they were always supportive of Gandhi's struggle for freedom and were willing to help.

With time, Saraswati's father became the owner of a gold mine in Rangoon but he always remained connected with developments in India and the movement for independence. One night, while the family was enjoying dinner with some guests, a sudden news on the radio changed the course of the evening. The newsreader announced the death sentence of Bhagat Singh. Her parents were terribly sad with this latest piece of information. Little Saraswati was too young to comprehend what had happened. She did not know who Bhagat Singh was and why he was getting hanged. The very next day she read about Bhagat Singh and the story of his courage and struggle in the newspaper. For her, it was a story like no other that she had ever heard.

Saraswati was deeply affected by this revolutionary leader. A feeling was born inside her that only total revolution can bring about independence, and ahimsa alone cannot secure it for us. Though her father kept talking about Mahatma Gandhi and the path of ahimsa, Saraswati could not agree with him and follow the path of Gandhi. Like Bhagat Singh, she too picked up a gun; in her heart, her targets were the British.

Saraswati was just ten years old when one day a special guest visited their home—he was none other than Mahatma Gandhi himself. Saraswati's father was a supporter of the Indian freedom movement and he used to send funds for the cause. So when Gandhi came to Rangoon, he visited them.

The whole household went into a tizzy to welcome such an important guest; everybody was excited, except little Saraswati. She was instead busy practising target shooting in the backyard. When Gandhi saw her with a gun in her hands, he was concerned. He advised her to shun the path of violence as it will only lead to destruction. Little Saraswati did not say anything to him but she wondered—what about the violence that the British do? Was that not wrong? Shouldn't they be punished for it?

Mahatma Gandhi had thousands of followers in India but he could not change the resolve of this ten-year-old girl. As soon as he left, she resumed her target shooting practice.

Only one leader stood up and openly spoke against the decision of hanging Bhagat Singh—Netaji Subhash Chandra Bose. His views were very different from Gandhi's. He did not believe in ahimsa but in direct action. His speeches were so powerful that Saraswati felt that he was the only one who could take on the British. She was deeply influenced by him and began collecting his pictures and speeches that were published in newspapers. Netaji was forming his army at that time as he believed that every nation that wanted to become independent should build its own army. He believed that even a country like Britain—where the sun never set in the empire—can also be defeated. In her heart, she made him her leader and waited to be a part of his army.

Netaji Subhash Chandra Bose

Gandhi and Netaji, before Netaji's eventual departure from the Congress

Netaji's personality was almost magical. Like a pied-piper he charmed the youth into joining his cause. In a district, a few hours from Rangoon, there was a sugar factory which was run by Indians from Bihar. They donated their sugar factory to Netaji's movement to help him in his movement. The men working there, their families, their wives, and their elderly parents—they all took part in Netaji's cause. Even the children used to love Netaji. This was due to his towering personality, the songs of Azad Hind and the dreams of independent India that he showed to them.

Saraswati used to memorize each and every word of Netaji's speech and then write it so as to remember it by heart. Every day she used to wait for Netaji to come to Rangoon so that she could meet him. At times, she would imagine what she would tell him when she got to meet him. Perhaps she would salute him with his own slogan 'Jai Hind!' She even started praying so that she could meet him.

Netaji wanted everybody—from a child to an elderly—to be a part of the battle for independence. His main strategy was to attack British-occupied India, and to achieve that he thought of an entry route via Kohima and Imphal. For a revolution to start within the country, he had established his network of spies, friends and companions across the country that he had sent from Singapore, Japan and Burma. These people came to India in 1942 and were waiting for Subhash Chandra Bose to come to the Indian border. Meanwhile, Japan supported Netaji by providing him with a section of the Japanese army which was headed by General Tojo. A Japanese force of about eighty thousand soldiers was with him. Netaji's own Azad Hind Fauj comprised forty thousand people, of which about thirty thousand were prisoners of war (PoWs). These PoWs were actually Indian men who had gone to fight for England in the war against Japan, but were captured. When the Japanese released them, Netaji persuaded them to be a part of his army. It was an unprecedented feat by Netaji to convince such a large army to switch sides and fight against their own government for the independence of their country. But it was a part of his brilliant strategy.

After a few months, while coming back from school one day, Saraswati heard that Netaji was coming to Rangoon. The slogans of 'Poorn Sangrahan' and 'Param Balidaan' which Netaji had started about twelve months back started to show their impact. He believed that the dream of an independent nation was about to become a reality. Saraswati recalled Netaji's speeches where he said that there should be only one desire at this point

SARASWATI RAJAMANI

Soldiers of the INA

of time—the desire to die so that Bharat (India) could live. He demanded the blood of his people because blood and only blood could pay the cost of freedom. He said, '*Tum mujhe khoon do, main tumhe azadi doonga*' (You give me blood, I will give you freedom). Saraswati was so impressed and excited after listening to Netaji's speeches that she wished to give her blood to him that very instant.

During this time, Netaji's camps were also collecting donation—whatever the people had to offer. Saraswati also went there to donate whatever she could. Since she was from a very rich family, she had a lot of gold and diamond jewellery which she gave away for Netaji's cause. The person collecting the donations was shocked. He asked her name and she told him that her name was Rajamani.

Once after the speech, Netaji was standing on the dais accepting donations from the people. People came forward with what they had: lakhs of money and even jewellery. There was a huge queue of donors when an old ragged-looking woman came with just two rupees in her hand. Trembling, she reached Netaji and offered what she had got. Netaji cast one look at her tattered self. His fellow fighter Shah Nawaz awaited Netaji's reaction. To his surprise, Netaji took that two rupees, touched it to his forehead and touched the woman's feet and accepted the money. That same night in their armoury camp, Shah Nawaz asked Netaji why he had taken that money from that old woman and whether those two rupees would actually make any difference. Netaji smiled and replied, 'It matters a lot, Shah Nawaz. That mother should not feel that her Netaji and this movement are only for the rich. She should feel that it is also of the poor; it is theirs too. For this I took that two rupee from her.'

SARASWATI RAJAMANI

One day when Saraswati reached home from school, someone was sitting with her father. It was Netaji! Saraswati was so awe-struck that she became speechless. The way Gandhi had visited the Rajamani household, in a similar way Netaji too had come visiting. He had come to return the jewellery she had donated at one of his camps for the movement. He gave it all back to her father and told him that his daughter had given it towards his cause but these were too valuable, and she should take it back. Saraswati was just sixteen at that time.

She protested saying it was her jewellery which she had given to Netaji, and he should not try to hand it over to her father. 'If you say that this movement belongs to everyone, then you will have to accept this jewellery,' she said. She added she would take the jewellery back on only one condition—that is, if he agrees to take her in his army. More than her education at school, at that time, she felt it was important to serve her country. Her father too understood this. Netaji told her that she was too young but she was adamant about contributing to his cause. She had waited too long for this moment and now she could not have let Netaji go without saying a yes. Ultimately, he agreed, and Saraswati's dream of becoming a soldier of the country began to take shape.

Netaji was left impressed by this young girl's insistence and passion about the cause of the independence of the country; to him it seemed that she was talking like Goddess Saraswati herself. He told her that while Goddess Lakshmi comes and goes, Goddess Saraswati if she comes once, she stays forever. He compared her to Saraswati and thus changed her name from Rajamani to Saraswati. Rajamani was the name she had got after her birth but Netaji gave her a new name, Saraswati.

Saraswati was first trained to be a nurse to look after the wounded soldiers of INA. To be alongside Netaji, she was willing to do everything. Her parents were happy that she was getting to learn so much. But the kind of girl that Saraswati was, she was not satisfied being just a nurse. She wanted to do something more exciting and daring while in the INA.

One day at the dispensary she saw an INA soldier talking to a British soldier and taking money from him. She was not working as a spy but she noticed such an exchange of information and currency and thought Netaji must know about it.

The INA soldier-training camp was about seven miles away from Rangoon. Saraswati used to love visiting it. There she saw many young people like her. It was her secret desire that Netaji should make her also a part of that camp. She wanted to prove that she can become a soldier for Netaji. She met and told Netaji what she had seen at the dispensary. Netaji immediately believed her and sent his men to inquire about it. At the same time, he realized that this girl can be put to better use than just nursing. He decided that she could join his camp and get trained. Saraswati could not believe her ears; this was what she had always wanted.

The training started soon. There were many girls like Saraswati in the camp who wanted to do something for their country. Trainees had to get up at four every morning; the training included how to use different types of rifles. They were trained for everything regarding how an enemy was to be confronted and how to fight in a war. Those days were definitely very difficult but the most memorable of Saraswati's life. No matter if it rained or if the sun blazed away, the training routine never changed. It was in this very camp that Saraswati met Durga. They were partners. They used to do everything together.

According to Dr Vishwas Patil, author of *Mahanayak* (2013), this was the time when Indian girls wore only saris, but at his camp Netaji gave them the uniform of a proper soldier. The women regiment of his army used to wear shirts and trousers. There is no doubt that Netaji was the first man in the world to form a women-only army. When the girls went to Maymyo (currently the town of Pyin Oo Lwin) in Burma, Netaji told them that though he had trained them to fight in a war and fire a gun, he could not tell them to start firing. At this, all the girls got together and cutting their fingers, they wrote a letter in blood to Netaji saying that he could take their collective judgement whether the girls would fight at the border or step back. This act impressed Netaji and he allowed a girls-only regiment to be established a little further from Maymyo, in Kohima and Imphal.

Some of the girls got recruited in the Rani Jhansi regiment. But Saraswati and Durga got selected for a special job by Netaji. For this special task they had to get their hair shortened. They did not know what to expect, but Netaji's instruction was most important to them. Both the girls got a makeover and they were made to appear like boys. Then Netaji informed them about their secret mission. He wanted both of them to work as his spies in the British camp. His confidence in them made Saraswati transform from his father's dearest daughter to a spy of the country.

SARASWATI RAJAMANI

Image of the Rani Jhansi regiment, 1940s

Netaji's spies were placed at two or three crucial locations: one was the actual Indo-Burma border. Indian soldiers working in the British army, who were officially fighting against Netaji, used to spy for him, as did some in the Japanese advanced force. Girls like Saraswati were sent for spying to the British camps and army cantonments as servants or postmen or as water bearers, and they used to get back valuable information from there.

Saraswati and Durga went to a British camp about 700 kilometres from Rangoon. They were brought there as office and helper boys. British camps were in constant need of such boys. When they were asked for their names, Saraswati said that her name was Mani. The office was already briefed that these 'boys' could clean and sweep and make food and would not give any chance of a complaint. Both the girls were very scared; what if the British got to know? What if they floundered and got caught? But they both got the job nevertheless.

They were majorly given routine housekeeping jobs such as laundry, polishing shoes and cleaning, but their actual job was to listen to everything the British officers said and to get all those information delivered to the INA camp. The INA was particularly interested in the British army's next step in the World War. Saraswati and Durga used to listen to every conversation very carefully. Gradually they became fearless in their endeavour. They would break locks and enter forbidden areas to get secret information. The danger of getting caught was always there but by then they had learnt how to save themselves.

While being in and around British camps, their ears were always alert on the lookout for more information. They used to collect whatever information they could get on strategy or war or anything else of use and pass it on to Netaji.

Netaji's spy system was wide and intricate. There were many ways to pass on information to him. The people of

Rangoon were also involved in Netaji's movement and were always ready to help the INA. In World War II, the members of the INA were fighting the war along with Japan, against the wishes of Gandhi. However, Netaji believed that the enemy's enemy is our friend.

As the days passed, the girls started taking more risks and even started stealing weapons. The INA needed weapons while the British had them in abundance. Netaji believed that the British were weak in their military resources at that time as they must have used them in fighting the war. If they were hit equally, from both inside and out, there was a chance of ousting them from the country. He was immensely appreciative of the girls' contribution. He used to say that all these small bits of information were playing a huge role in the war. He had acknowledged that the girls were doing a dangerous job, living right there in the enemy's den. If they were ever to be caught, their death was inevitable. However, it was everybody's collective responsibility to make Netaji's dream come true.

A year had gone by when one day Durga was caught peeping around. Saraswati should have run away right then but her mind went numb in shock. She could not understand what she should do. She was terrified, but being a strong girl, she did not lose her good sense.

Saraswati felt that Durga and she were partners all along and now she could not leave her there alone, while escaping on her own. She resolved to free her friend. She disguised herself as a cleaner, wearing a local dress, and went to the jail where Durga was imprisoned. Durga had been crying inside her cell. When Durga looked at her, she gestured her to stay quiet though she herself was very scared. The plan could have all gone wrong if that officer had suspected them even a bit. Saraswati's co-cleaner splashed water around the room, forcing the officer to move out. As soon as he stepped out, Saraswati went to Durga. There was no time to exchange words. The priority was to set Durga free. She tried to open the lock of her cell with her hairpin but it wasn't easy. After a few more tries, she succeeded and took Durga out.

There was no time to think. They had to take this risk. Taking Netaji's name, both the girls ran from the jail. They ran as fast as they could. But they were not faster than the bullet fired at them. Saraswati got shot in the leg. She urged Durga to run away but Durga said, 'If we run, we run together. If we die, we die together.' There was a moment of absolute understanding and a rush of energy. They started running again, as fast as they could and went inside the jungle. They climbed atop a tree and hid themselves there. Had somebody asked them later they would not have been able to tell how they had managed to climb the tree in that state.

Blood was flowing from Saraswati's wound. For a soldier, a bullet wound is like a medal but at that moment she could only feel the pain and the fear. For three days, the girls sat atop that tree. They were scared to come down as they feared being caught again. On the fourth day, they somehow found more courage and got down. Saraswati could not feel her leg which was shot. They both consoled each other and tried to regain some strength. They had a lot of distance to cover and they were still not out of danger. Saraswati was about to give up. She was missing her parents too. She was scared about how much more would she able to endure. She was also afraid that if they got lost in the jungle, no one would ever get to know what had happened to them. Netaji's words and his love for the nation had got internalized in the girls. They did not want to disappoint him. They had to reach Rangoon anyhow.

After an arduous eight-hour journey, they reached Rangoon and then somehow managed to drag themselves to their camp. As soon as they stepped inside, they fell on the ground exhausted. Their comrades at INA were surprised to see them. They had presumed them dead. They had heard of Durga's capture and Saraswati getting shot at. But on reaching the camp, the girls were not afraid of anything anymore. They were home.

A few days later Saraswati got a letter from Netaji. He congratulated her on her exemplary courage. He also wrote that such acts of bravery keep reminding him the cause of his fight. They were probably the youngest spies of India; they were only sixteen at that time. Saraswati read and reread that letter many times. More than happiness, it gave her solace that they had not disappointed him.

And then the day arrived, when India got its freedom. Everything had happened the way Netaji had foretold. On 15 August 1947, the British government handed the reins of the country to its people and left it forever. Unfortunately, Netaji did not survive to witness this historical event. Two years before that, on 18 August 1945, he had died in a Japanese plane crash in Taiwan. Nobody could believe that he was no more; so his people kept waiting for him. There was no other person who could lead the INA after his death and that's how the soldiers of Azad Hind Fauj got disbanded. Saraswati too returned to India with her family at the age of twenty.

It is indeed unfortunate that the Azad Hind Fauj never received as much credit for its sacrifices as it deserved. Even after twenty-five years of Indian Independence, till 1971, the people who had fought along with Netaji in the Azad Hind Fauj were not even given the title of freedom fighters.

Presently, Saraswati lives in Chennai, India. When she spoke to Shobha Warrier in an interview, she showed the same amount of excitement and enthusiasm talking about her Rangoon days and experience with Netaji. The same passion seemed missing when she spoke about the rest of her life. But she was disappointed that despite doing so much for the country, she got neither recognition nor appreciation. This was a major cause of her sadness. A woman who had shown unparalleled courage and endurance for her country, who had fought in the war for freedom, today in her twilight years, she has sadness in her eyes. If someone asks who is responsible for that, Warrier says, we as a nation have failed her.

Saraswati says, 'Netaji had given me a letter but while coming back to India, the custom officers took everything of mine. I was not even left with clothes to wear. This is what they did to me. My name is Rajamani. Netaji had given me the name Saraswati. Jai Hind!'

Saraswati Rajamani, Chennai, 2016

EXPERTS

Shobha Warrier is the associate editorial director at Rediff.com. She met and interviewed Saraswati Rajamani.

Vishwas Patil is an award-winning author. He is known widely for his research and is the author of *Mahanayak*.

10

Rameshwar N. Kao and K. Shankaran Nair

RAW Spies and the 1971 War
(1971)

The external intelligence agency of India—the Research and Analysis Wing (RAW)—considers the separation of Bangladesh from West Pakistan in 1971 as one of its biggest operations till date. At the head of the mission was Rameshwar N. Kao, the first chief of the RAW, and his number two man, K. Shankaran Nair (K.S.N.). While the operation was on from the early months of 1970, the actual war for liberation is known to have lasted all of thirteen days in December 1971. The reason behind the successful operation was a large network of intelligence organizations working in tandem across India, including the training of Mukti Bahini, which was created from the East Pakistan refugees who had entered Indian borders. While still in its earliest days, Kao and K.S.N. managed to put together a brilliant team of men who were trained in guerilla warfare and weakened the presence of West Pakistan soldiers in Bangladesh before the actual Indian army could even enter the field of action. While Kao planned from New Delhi, K.S.N. was involved in the field. Known among the East Pakistan rebels as Col. Menon, K.S.N. was involved in training refugees into a fierce army that brought down the West Pakistan army and managed to gain independence for Bangladesh.

Running a spy organization is not one man's job. There are several links attached to it: a network of people, a lot of machinery and money, and intensive planning.

After the Sino-Indian war in 1962 and the Indo-Pak war in 1965, the Government of India realized that the functioning of the Intelligence Bureau (IB), which till then used to collect foreign information, was not satisfactory. It was decided then that to do this job a separate organization was required. Thus was born

RAW, which was constituted in 1968 as the primary foreign intelligence agency of India. The main task of this organization was to stay one step ahead of the enemy nations and keep an eye on their movements. The agency was new but its intelligence network was not. They were not field agents; they were spy masters and their job was to always stay a step ahead of the enemy.

R.N. Kao and K.S.N., members of RAW, worked very hard to build the agency network, and when on 3 March 1971, a phone call was tapped they knew that their hard work had paid off.

In the 1940s, when the clamour for dividing the country on religious lines was growing, nobody thought of how the Muslim-majority East Bengal would fit in the idea of Pakistan that was being discussed. But when Pakistan was being carved out, Mohammad Ali Jinnah, the future father of the nation of Pakistan, thought of including East Bengal as well in the map of Pakistan. That way, Pakistan would be a big country and in future if there was ever a clash with India, then it would be in a position to give an equal fight from both sides of the border.

Within a year of Pakistan's independence in 1947,

Prime Minister Mohammad Ali Jinnah passed away. Even before his death, tension had spread its roots between the two parts of Pakistan—West and East. According to A.K. Verma, former chief of RAW, fifty-five per cent of the Pakistani population was in East Pakistan which spoke Bangla. This was a heavy percentage of people who did not speak Urdu, unlike West Pakistan. However, the Government of Pakistan declared Urdu as the national language (Urdu was also spoken in Uttar Pradesh, Bihar and Madhya Pradesh in India). The areas which comprised West Pakistan—Punjab, Balochistan, Sindh and Frontier Province—did not speak Urdu as well. But the Pakistan government decided that there should be a single official language and they made Urdu their national language.

The Bengalis in East Pakistan protested against this decision and stated that they would not accept Urdu. As Bangla-speaking people were in majority in Pakistan, they demanded that Bangla should be made the national language. The leaders from West Pakistan did not agree to this demand. This issue kicked up a huge political storm.

Syed Nazrul Islam, a Bangladeshi politician and a senior leader of the Awami League, said, 'Just after partition, a stunning blow came when the rulers, who came to power in the central government, declared that Urdu shall be the only state language of Pakistan.'

Syed Ali Ahsan, a Bangladeshi poet, writer and professor, said, 'Language has its own history. Like human beings language grows automatically. And you cannot create a language and you cannot change the complexion of language by imposition.'

The people of East Pakistan were waiting for the martial law, which started in 1969, to come to an end. They were waiting for an end to their continuous exploitation by the army generals and some affluent families of West Pakistan. When the abuse became too much, the Bengalis protested. Sheikh Mujibur Rahman, then a prominent leader of the Awami League (who later served twice as Bangladesh's president) came forward to lead the Bengalis. His nationalist movement was based on six points, but his main demands were that elections should be held under parliamentary form of democracy and that East and West Pakistan should be given the status of two different states. The purpose of it was that apart from defence and foreign affairs, East Pakistan should get the right of swarajya (independent state), especially where the economy was concerned.

Sheikh Mujibur Rahman

Sheikh Mujibur Rahman said, 'As the central government missionaries are there in West Pakistan...as the central administration is in the hands of West Pakistanis...as the military installations and military personnel come from West Pakistan and the ten per cent from Bengal in the armed forces and fifteen per cent in the central administration. Naturally, these twenty-two years you have seen that East Pakistan here, particularly Bengal, is nothing but a colonial market.'

There was a monopoly of jute in East Pakistan and its export generated huge amount of income. But a very small portion of this income was used for East Pakistan and the major part went into the development of West Pakistan.

General Yahya Khan, the third president of Pakistan, on the issue of withdrawing martial law and conducting election, said, 'My intention [of] remaining a president has nothing to do with me. The person of democracy and the government will elect their president. And unless I offer myself for that election, I can't remain a president and I am not offering myself to be president.'

In December 1970, on the basis of universal adult franchise, elections were conducted. The secular nature of Awami League became the main reason of its victory in the general elections. In the Pakistan General Assembly, out of 313 seats, East Pakistan secured 169 seats, out of which Awami League won 167 seats. And thus, Sheikh Mujibur Rahman became the unopposed leader, elected with absolute majority in the National Assembly of Pakistan.

However, though Sheikh Mujib's party had got the majority in both the wings of Pakistan, West Pakistan would not have allowed him to be the prime minister at any cost.

Before 1971, at no public event had Mujibur Rahman stated that he wanted East Bengal to become an independent nation. But when the seat of the prime minister was denied to him, that probably was the first time when he must have thought of demanding secession and becoming an independent nation.

Meanwhile, Zulfikar Ali Bhutto, who was the leader of Pakistan's People Party (PPP), had got a majority in West Pakistan. He threatened to boycott the Assembly. He demanded a change in the Constitution which stated that the majority party could not bring about any amendment in it, without the consent of the minority party. The Assembly got suspended till 25 March 1971.

Around the same time, Indian agents noticed some kind of movement on the encrypted communication channels of West Pakistan. They were also keeping a sharp eye on Pakistan's administration and military movements. They assumed correctly that the Pakistan army had no intention of allowing democracy in East Pakistan. They were tapping as many phones which were ringing across the border. There were gossips that the postponement of the Assembly was just an eyewash, a drama to secure more time, and a part of this drama was the negotiations happening between Awami League and PPP. Meanwhile, the people of East Pakistan were losing patience. Sheikh Mujib requested the citizens to exercise their democratic rights. Respecting the demands of the citizens, he announced a non-cooperation movement against the Government of Pakistan.

Intelligence at that point had two aspects. One was the overall strategic intelligence, under which the East Pakistan issue had to be decided—how the region can be made more stable—and the other was operational intelligence, under which came the information of what the Pakistan army was doing and how to extract that classified information. Very soon, Indian intelligence officers got to know that the army officers sitting in Lahore Club were planning the arrest of Mujibur Rahman.

Ever since the result of the National Assembly elections, Bhutto's stand was that he would never accept Bengali superiority under any condition; this had become public knowledge. The Government of Pakistan soon started oppressing Bengalis by using force. They increased their army presence in East Pakistan, which till then was concentrated largely in West Pakistan. A whole division—Division Number 9—was airlifted from West to East Pakistan. Tanks were also moved and so was heavy military.

Both RAW and IB worked together during the

operations of 1971. India had always known that Sheikh Mujibur Rahman wanted to collaborate with India; so Indian officers were already in touch with him. Very soon Indian intelligence confirmed that the Pakistan army was planning something big in East Pakistan. K.S.N. immediately called Kao and told him that Pakistanis were planning the oppression of Bengalis in East Pakistan. Kao decided to go to East Pakistan himself. He tried to reason with Sheikh Mujib that his arrest plan had been made and a whole division of the Pakistan army had left for East Pakistan. Kao suggested to him that he should go underground as his life was in danger. Sheikh Mujib knew that he could become the target of Pakistani bullets any day, but he also knew that he could not leave his country in that hour of trial.

The Indian agents wanted to take a firm step to stop the Pakistanis. When Indian Prime Minister Indira Gandhi asked Field Marshal Sam Manekshaw as to what could be done to stop the Pakistanis, he asked for six months' time. Though it was actually Pakistan's internal affair and it did not suit India to interfere, the government knew that if a civil war erupted in Pakistan, the one nation that would get directly affected was India.

Meanwhile, the Pakistani leadership started considering options of stopping the movement. They permitted their army, and organizations like the Razakar, to selectively kill people. They selected and murdered intellectual Bengalis from all fields—universities professors and school teachers, lawyers, doctors and engineers—and even military and government officers. Anybody who posed even a remote threat of leading the civilian movement was threatened or ordered to be killed.

Things happened exactly the way RAW officials had anticipated. The Pakistan army stamped and crushed the wave of Bengali nationalism. But in spite of knowing everything, India could do nothing. Matters of politics always take time, especially when the matter was about the destiny of a whole country and involved cross-border tension.

As violence mounted, people left their homes in East Pakistan and migrated to India through West Bengal, Bihar, Assam, Tripura and Meghalaya. Everyday almost forty thousand refugees trooped into India from across the border. It was not easy to provide refuge to lakhs of migrants and the Indian government came under tremendous pressure. Even the most affluent countries would give up taking care of the basic needs of such a

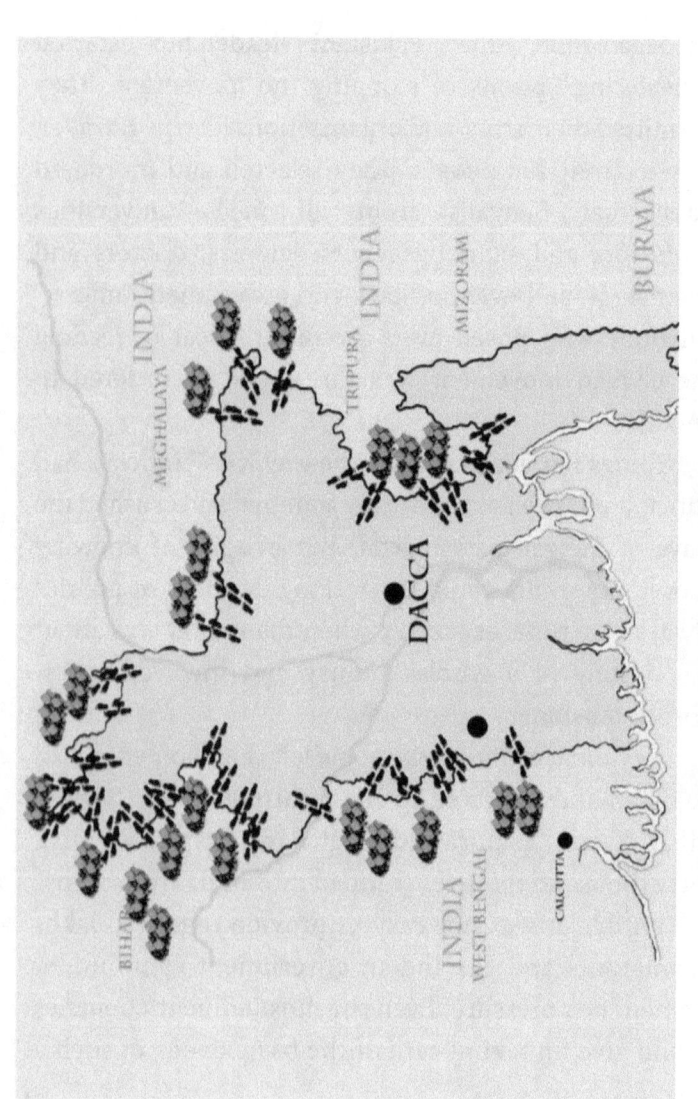

Map of East Pakistan depicting the migration to India

large number of refugees. In a single camp in Kolkata, there were two and a half lakh people and feeding them every day was becoming an impossible task. During this time, many international organizations came forward in support of the Indian government in this endeavour. By the end of 1971, the count of influx of Bangladeshi refugees had crossed ten lakh. This was more than the total population of Belgium, Saudi Arabia and Iraq.

Time had now come to approach other governments for a strategy to contain this influx and manage this international development. Prime Minister Indira Gandhi signed a Treaty of Security and Mutual Cooperation with Russia. She also went on a tour to the West. She first visited the USA and Europe, and asked her counterparts there for assistance. She urged them to put pressure on Pakistan. But Richard Nixon, the then US president, was not ready to listen and refused any help. So in a way, the Indian government was left in the lurch and was forced to find a solution to the problem on its own. Decisions had to be taken and they had to be taken soon.

In a television interview, Indira Gandhi said, 'Do you think people are going to sit aside and watch their women raped in front of them? And say that you know we are going to quieten the situation? That's not quietness. That is the worst possible type of war. It's the worst possible type of violence.'

While all these atrocities were going on, the leaders of East Pakistan fled; they came to India and started living near Kolkata. Very soon, they became the government-in-exile and started pressurizing India to help them in some way. They argued that India could see the way they were being oppressed; so the government should do something to stop the Pakistan army's oppression.

On the morning of 17 April 1971, in a small village in Kushtia district, at a mango orchard, the formulation of Democratic Republic of Bangladesh was officially announced. The Pakistan army had already arrested Mujibur Rahman and had taken him to an undisclosed location. People were afraid that he might have been killed. In his absence, Vice President Syed Nasrul Islam became the acting president.

For strategic intelligence, India supported the independent government of Sheikh Mujibur Rahman in West Bengal and made a base for them. They formed a force named Mukti Bahini which got trained in tactics and leadership, working with the Indian army. Thousands of Bengali volunteers started coming to the camps along with East Pakistan Rifles and East Bengal Regiment and other paramilitary forces. This army of Mukti Datas (providers of freedom) was later known as Mukti Bahini. In six weeks India provided training to more than two thousand freedom fighters. The count was to increase every six weeks by over two thousand and it continued to go on till the Pakistan army surrendered at the end of the year. India did all this on the demand of the Awami movement and the people of East Pakistan. Mukti Bahini had become more powerful than before. India's weapons and training were increasing their morale and strengthening their hands.

It was not easy to control the training and coordination of Mukti Bahini. It was a joint operation among the Indian army, IB and RAW, and for those very reasons K.S.N. had to visit those camps. While the Mukti Bahini was getting trained, he adopted a fictitious name of Col. Menon. In the intelligence work, it is of utmost importance that your identity should not be known; so a fictitious name is a must.

Members in training, Mukti Bahini

The border between India and East Pakistan was 3,909 kilometres long. While on the one hand thousands of refugees were crossing over to India, on the other hand, Mukti Bahini soldiers trained by India were getting back across the border, but in small groups. Their aim was only the freedom of East Bengal.

Some officers went as coconut-sellers, some as grocery shop owners and in disguises like these, hundreds of them were sent inside East Pakistan. After entering the other side of the border, they started gathering intelligence while working in collaboration with the Mukti Bahini, and kept passing on information to Indian intelligence.

Refugees from East Pakistan, escaping to India

Relief camps for East Pakistan refugees, help pouring in from the Government of India

Indian agents were everywhere. Even the war room of Pakistan army was not out of their reach. Agents were located at such strategic places in West Pakistan that they could even give information about Pakistan's air force; there were men who had information about tank positions and the movement of divisions towards the border.

On the field, one day K.S.N. got a crucial information from one of his officers. The news could be a turning point in the war. The information was that the Pakistan air force had been ordered to do a sudden strike on forward air bases of India. The intelligence agent reported that the strike would take place in the next seventy-two hours. Also, it seemed that even a date was indicated—2 December.

According to protocol, K.S.N. gave the news to the dispatch officer. It was he who handled communication between the different departments of the government. The dispatch officer sent that important news in a sealed courier to the Indian air force.

So when the chiefs of air force and other defence arms were informed that a possible attack could take place on 2 December, everybody was on alert. But nothing happened on that particular date. Later it appeared that there may have been a confusion in Delhi regarding the interpretations of the information about the attack. This made the air force chief a bit upset. He said that his men were waiting on standby and asked how long they would be required to sit like that as it was very strenuous. He was then advised to wait for another twenty-four hours, as the attack alert was for the span of seventy-two hours, and there was still some time left. The date given was only indicative but fortunately he agreed.

After all, it was a piece of very important news that K.S.N. had got beforehand. Because of this input, the Indian air force could get their planes behind the frontier line. So when the attack by Pakistan started on 3 December, they could not do much damage. Also, when they tried to air drop their commandos around Halwara, most of them were caught.

Finally, on 3 December, Pakistani bombers bombed several Indian airfields and this was the mistake India was waiting for Pakistan to make. India was absolutely ready to fight this war with Pakistan. Everything happened exactly as informed. Within seventy-two hours, the Pakistan air force attacked the Indian air bases. The Indian forces were ready, and a ferocious war was fought for fourteen days. The Indian army and air force together gave a suitable reply to Pakistan, both in the East and West.

Every house in every village of East Bengal became a fort. Whether it was a student or a farmer, they fought like a soldier and gave the Pakistan army a befitting reply. The time had come for the end of Pakistani oppression of Bengalis. On the one hand, the Pakistan army was struggling with the juggernaut of the Indian army, and on the other, the Mukti Bahini soldiers were killing them one after another. Very soon, the Pakistani soldiers started to lose ground.

The Ninth Mountain Division of the Indian army had already declared victory in Jessore. The next concern was how to reach Dhaka (then called Dacca). A very daring decision was taken for it. Fifty paratroopers were airdropped behind enemy lines, where they were joined by the soldiers of Mukti Bahini; together they surrounded Dhaka from all sides. The Pakistan army had no choice but to surrender. At four o'clock on 16 December 1971, Lt. Gen. A.A.K. Niazi signed on the instrument of surrender and surrendered before Lt. Col. K.S. Aurora. The Indian army was welcomed like heroes at Dhaka.

According to A.K. Verma, former chief of RAW, East Pakistan had to become Bangladesh. It was in its destiny. It's a different matter that they got some help from India in it because the circumstances had become such that India had no other option but to help out East Pakistan. Till March 1971, nobody in India or Pakistan had any inkling that Bangladesh would be formed. But circumstances deteriorated so fast that the eastern part of Pakistan broke away by the end of the year and established itself as an independent state—the new nation of Bangladesh.

Bangladesh had now become an independent nation in the true sense. But even then the citizens of Bangladesh were eagerly waiting for the return of their leader, Sheikh Mujibur Rahman.

In her speech to the newly created state of Bangladesh and her citizens, Indira Gandhi said, 'In India, we had made three promises [to] our citizens. The first was that all refugees who had come here will go back. Second, we will help Mukti Bahini in every way possible. We will help the people of Bangladesh. And third, we will definitely get Sheikh Sahib released from the jail.'

The success of this war is a sample of the achievement of intelligence gathering, which usually doesn't get a mention after a victory.

Kao felt sad that they could not save the thousands

who were butchered by Pakistan in this war. But he was happy that because of them, lakhs of people were breathing in free air and were now citizens of a free country. Bangladesh was independent, and Bengalis had got the right now to write their own destiny.

Two men from RAW who deserve special mention for the success of the 1971 war are Rameshwar (Ramji or R.N.) Kao and K. Shankaran Nair. K.S.N. had the following to say about his former boss:

> [There was a] need for an external intelligence agency in India [so as] to prevent other agencies coming and becoming sneaks on us. Mr Kao was the brain behind organizing intelligence in the country for use against agents working against India.

EXPERTS

A.K. Verma was the RAW chief in the early 1990s. He continues to contribute articles on intelligence and security to defence forums.

K. Shankaran Nair was one of the earliest members of RAW. He was made the RAW chief in 1977 but retired in the same year, reportedly as a protest against the government.

www.ingramcontent.com/pod-product-compliance
Lightning Source LLC
Chambersburg PA
CBHW020354170426
43200CB00005B/169